Hunger For Wholeness

Poetry by D.H. Lawrence
Selected and Interpreted
By
Don Jones

Bloomington, IN Milton Keynes, UK

authorHOUSE®

AuthorHouse™
1663 Liberty Drive,
Suite 200
Bloomington, IN 47403
www.authorhouse.com
Phone: 1-800-839-8640

AuthorHouse™ UK Ltd.
500 Avebury Boulevard
Central Milton Keynes, MK9 2BE
www.authorhouse.co.uk
Phone: 08001974150

First published by AuthorHouse7/2/2007

ISBN: 978-1-4343-0940-2 (sc)
ISBN: 978-1-4343-0939-6 (hc)

Library of Congress Control Number: 2007902997

Printed in the United States of America
Bloomington, Indiana

This book is printed on acid-free paper.

All quotations of D.H. Lawrence's poetry are from *The Complete Poems of D.H. Lawrence*, published as a part of The Wordsworth Poetry Library, first published in 1994 by Wordsworth Editions Limited Cumberland House, Crib Street, Ware, Hertfordshire SG12 9ET, used by permisssion.

"Lawrence" is from *Donkey Gospel: Poems* by Tony Hoagland, Graywolf Press, 1998 and is used by permission.

Appendix A, "Life of D.H. Lawrence" by Petri Liukkonen, is from "Author's Calendar", http://www.kirjasto.sci.fi/, 2005 and is used by permission.

Acknowledgements

One of the joys of writing a book comes from the supportive relationship with a number of people who give encouragement to you during the struggles to get it into print.

My wife, Emily Hurst-Jones, was my first reader and her enthusiastic response gave me energy and will to keep going till done. My friend, Burtton Woodruff, used his influence to secure a study carrel at Butler University in which I could find the privacy and inspiration to write.

I am grateful to Lewis Miller, the Dean of Irwin Library at Butler, for his permission to occupy the space all summer.

My friend, Steven Judith, and my son, Jon Jones, were both indispensable in the proper formatting and preparation of the manuscript. Bill Lennon's generosity and Henry Kreutzinger's support have kept me moving forward in spite of self-doubts.

Dennis Hart of Wordsworth Limited Publishers gave permission to use over 30 poems from their edition of the Complete Poems of D.H. Lawrence. His clarification of permission questions was invaluable.

JR Harris of Author House Publishers has provided much needed expertise in moving forward with publication.

All these people stand behind whatever success this book may have, and I am deeply grateful.

Table of Contents

There are vast realms of consciousness still undreamed of vast ranges of experience, like the humming of unseen harps, we know nothing of, within us.

D.H. Lawrence—"Terra Incognita"

Introduction

Poetry is ecstatic speech. It is intended to be spoken aloud, not simply read silently from the page. D.H. Lawrence's poetry is ecstatic in nature, particularly his poems which are concerned with issues of human wholeness.

As a keynote speaker at conferences, I have derived great joy from introducing D.H. Lawrence's poetry.

Often I have asked the audience to stand and repeat the poems line by line at the top of their voices. At the close of such poems as "Escape," "Healing" or "Lizard," spoken aloud as a kind of litany, the energy in the crowd of people has built to a crescendo truly wonderful to hear.

I have seen few scenes in my life as impressive as these. I have heard few sounds as inspiring. I have loved few moments in my life as profoundly. I have experienced few rituals as effective in producing ecstatic joy or insight.

My vision for writing this book has been simply to introduce some of D.H. Lawrence's magnificent poems in such a way that others might come to love and appreciate them as I do. People from every walk of life can find enjoyment and inspiration from Lawrence's poetry, and I invite them all to join me as I seek to reveal the depth and beauty of the work of a man whom I believe was a true genius in understanding the deep places of the human heart. The poetry introduced in this book can truly help human beings re-discover and celebrate their deeper nature.

I first heard a D.H. Lawrence poem read aloud at an Indiana Men's Gathering in September of 1990. Robert Bly, the renowned poet, and Robert Moore, co-author of the great work about men, *King,*

Warrior, Magician, Lover, were the conference leaders. I don't recall which of them read Lawrence's poem "Escape," with the sounds of the sitar and tabla in the background, but the impact on me was profound and left me with a hunger to know more about D.H. Lawrence and his poetry.

As soon as the conference was over, I purchased my first copy of *The Complete Poems* by D.H. Lawrence and reveled in successive discoveries of stirring pieces of poetry embodying the energy of human struggle and triumph. I still have that book, tattered and worn from travel over the world and from frequent use in conferences of all kinds. It is now an icon in my library and I will surely cherish it for the rest of my life.

Of all the poems in this book, well over 200 of them deal with the challenges and changes faced by men and women in our modern age. I have used only thirty-five of these poems in the present volume, but they are sufficient to convince my readers to explore the whole body of Lawrence's poetry. At least, that is my fondest hope.

D.H. Lawrence was born September 11, 1885, in the little coal-mining village of Eastwood, nestled in the Erewash Valley, eight miles northwest of Nottingham, England, the nearest town of any size. Going deep into the earth to mine coal became for Lawrence a powerful metaphor of going deep into the human unconscious to discover its riches.

Who was D.H. Lawrence and what did he stand for? The answer is in one way very simple. He stood for the wholeness of the human individual as the final aim and goal of existence. He fought against every form of collective minimization of the individual. Even in marriage he holds out for individuality. He would not agree that marriage was some form of superior or substitute wholeness.

He believed moreover that an author or thinker needed to produce his ideas out of the whole depths of his soul rather than from mere mental reflection. He affirmed that true thought comes as much from the heart and the genitals, as the head. He held that an author should not be above the heads of the people talking down to them in some supposed superiority. He believed that an author should be in among the crowd, kicking their rear ends or encouraging them to some adventure or challenge. He was determined that his readers would be in the thick of life, and if they didn't like it, they could read someone else.

D.H. Lawrence was the first author to use the insights of Freud's and Jung's depth psychology in English novels. This same sense of the mysterious depths in human nature comes through mightily in his poetry.

Moreover, Lawrence's religious convictions were a crucial part of his life and literary work. His individualism was not so radical as to exclude a need for connection with the *great world*, or the larger life of the universe which he spoke of in such tones as to reveal a deeply spiritual relationship to it.

There was a time in the not too distant past when D.H. Lawrence was anathema to academic circles. His strong emphasis on the importance of masculine energy and leadership ran counter to the dramatic increase of women's studies departments in almost all the major universities. Lawrence scholars were hard-pressed to maintain their status in the struggle for an important place in the academic sun.

However, the tide is turning again toward a serious consideration of Lawrence as one of the greatest British novelists and men of letters. In particular, many major poets are rising to the challenge of re-establishing the importance of his poetic work as the founder of a new kind of poetic genre, that of *romantic modernism*.

I have written this book in the hopes that it might, in some small way, do honor to the greatness of D.H. Lawrence, and also inspire many to explore more deeply the wonders of his poetry and prose.

I want to share a delightful poem in which the rise to D.H. Lawrence's defense is depicted in a most memorable way. This poem appeared in the volume of *The Best American Poetry of 1999*. Author, Tony Hoagland, has published several books of his own poetry and is now a professor at the University Of Houston. Enjoy!

Lawrence

On two occasions in the past twelve months
I have failed when someone at a party
spoke of him with a dismissive scorn,
to stand up for D.H. Lawrence.

a man who burned like an acetylene torch
from one end to the other of his life.
These individuals, whose relationship to literature
is approximately that of a tree shredder

to stands of old-growth forest,
these people leaned back in their chairs,
bellies full of dry white wine and the ovum of some foreign fish,
and casually dropped his name

the way pygmies with their little poison spears
strut around the carcass of a fallen elephant.
"O Elephant," they say,
"you are not so big and brave today!"

It's a bad day when people speak of their superiors
with a contempt they haven't earned,
and it's a sorry thing when certain other people

don't defend the great dead ones
who have opened up the world before them.
And though, in the catalogue of my betrayals,
this is a fairly minor entry,

I resolve, if the occasion should recur,
to uncheck my tongue and say; "I love the spectacle
of maggots condescending to a corpse,"
or, "You should be so lucky in your brainy, bloodless life

as to deserve to lift
just one of D.H. Lawrence's urine samples
to your arid psychobiographic
theory-tainted lips."

Or maybe I'll just take the shortcut
between the spirit and the flesh,
and punch someone in the face,
because human beings haven't come that far

in their effort to subdue the body,
and we still walk around like zombies
in our dying, burning world,
able to do little more

than fight, and fuck, and crow,
something Lawrence wrote about
in such a manner
as to make us seem magnificent.

Human Liberation

Escape

When we get out of the glass bottles of our own ego,
and when we escape like squirrels from turning in the
       cages of our personality
and get into the forest again,
we shall shiver with cold and fright
but things will happen to us
so that we don't know ourselves.

Cool, unlying life will rush in,
and passion will make our bodies taut with power,
we shall stamp our feet with new power
and old things will fall down,
we shall laugh, and institutions will curl up like burnt paper. .

Riches

When I wish I was rich, then I know I am ill.
Because, to tell the truth, I have enough as I am.
So when I catch myself thinking: Ah, if I was rich!
I say to myself: Hello! I'm not well. My vitality is low.

We human beings are trapped inside our own egos. We can only see what our ego-tainted eyes allow us to see. We can only feel what our limited egos permit us to sense. We can only experience what our cautious egos perceive to be safe.

Our controlling egos have made a decision about the size of the world we can live in and anything outside the boundaries of that pre-determined realm is either too irrelevant or too dangerous to merit our attention.

So, says the poet, we are like squirrels in a cage that can be very excited and animated but unable to experience novelty, change, or adventure. Our ego is the deciding part of ourselves. Our personality, on the other hand, is the expressive part of ourselves. Lawrence is saying both sides of us are trapped - the ego in a glass bottle which provides maximum display but no freedom—the personality in a squirrel cage that turns as fast as we want but takes us nowhere except in an interminable circle.

Our only hope is escape. The possibility of escape lies buried in our archaic memory of the time when we were not so domesticated, safe, and controlled. We have a faint, yet distinct memory that we were not always so enclosed. We used to live in the forest and the forest was hardly a comfort zone. It was full of mystery, unexpected thrills and dangers that kept us fully alive. The forest is our original, natural home where our own wild, mysterious nature can resonate with the surrounding uncertainties and challenges.

When we are able to *get into the forest again* we reclaim something of who we are, something we lost long ago as we became more civilized and self-protective.

All our efforts to make life warm and cozy are taking us away from our original nature. We were born to risk, to adventure, to make our way in the wilderness around us by using all our wit and wisdom, wiliness and skill. How long has it been since our last visit to this awesome place where our real humanity is awakened and stimulated?

When we go there again, our carefully controlled emotions will no longer prevail. *New and powerful feelings will grip us. We shall shiver with cold and fright.* A shiver is an involuntary convulsion of our muscles, indeed, our whole body, and it lets us know we are now outside the realm of ego-control. We are seized by an autonomic response, a shock of primitive feeling that overrides our calm, relaxed grip on ourselves.

The shiver of cold and fright is the pre-condition for discovery. Usually nothing new can happen until our complacency is shattered by some overpowering emotion that opens all the doors of perception.

Then *things will happen to us so that we don't know ourselves.* Our existing self-knowledge will be so suddenly expanded that it will feel like an explosion of who we were. The carefully constructed ego-boundaries and personality cages are cracked wide open like an egg shell that can no longer contain or restrain the burgeoning newness that will not be denied.

Once the modern human being escapes the ego-bottle and the personality-cage, a flood of new life will be released. The transformation will not take long. The energy for it will come from a depth beyond the normal boundaries of the self. Lawrence calls this new energy "cool, unlying life." It does not creep or seep, but rushes in and overwhelms the false ego-posturing and the phony personality-display that we humans substitute for our naturally true selfhood.

Our poet was convinced that the human dilemma exists because we believe and accept the lies we are told. The dual sources of these lies are other people and our societal culture. We are told lies about ourselves when we are young, and we believe them. The lies can either depress or inflate us, but in either case our acceptance of them creates in us a false self-image.

If we are told we are "not good enough" or "will never amount to much", then we will adopt a low self-image that guarantees life-long depression and failure of nerve. If, on the other hand, we are told we are "special" and we are surrounded by admiration and privilege, we manifest a life-long grandiosity and narcissism. In either case, our acceptance of the lies we are told about ourselves puts our ego in a bottle and our personality in a cage which Lawrence images as our human predicament.

Not only do people lie to us, but also our culture at large. While the people-lies are about our personal nature and potential, the culture-lies are about the meaning of life and what its ultimate goal must be.

Our poet's reading of this culture-lie is very clear. He states it in a short, shocking phrase—"Get money or eat dirt!" ("Being Alive") This is the meaning of modern life. The whole culture of the western world is based on the goal of economic aggrandizement. When we accept this lie, we become fatally alienated from our true selves and the wholeness of who we are.

Instead of realizing our true greatness, we become less than human in our effort to *get money*. We become *monkeys minding machines*. Whether the machine is a single lathe in a factory or a large corporate institution doesn't matter, our servitude is clearly the doom of our humanity. The love of money and the desire to be rich is the terminal illness of the human race. Lawrence put it in his telling little poem entitled "Riches."

> *When I wish I was rich, then I know I am ill.*
> *Because, to tell the truth, I have enough as I am.*
> *So when I catch myself thinking: Ah, if I was rich!*
> *I say to myself: Hello! I'm not well. My vitality is low.*

Our deliverance from *lying life* is to find our way into the forest again. Find the place of adventure and risk where *new things will happen to us, so that we don't know ourselves.* In other words, we quit believing the lies we are told and plunge into the forest of discovery where we may reclaim our original selves and get to know the *god-self* we were created to be. We reject the culture lies and start living a life not based on wages, nor profits, nor any sort of buying and selling, but on a religion of life.

Once we experience the rush of *cool, unlying life* we will find a force of life driving us forward into the newness of passion. Even our physical bodies will be revitalized by this force. Here is how Lawrence says it,

> *And passion will make our bodies taut with power,*
> *we shall stamp our feet with new power*
> *and old things will fall down,*

Now we see what we have lost by our acceptance of lies: our passion and power to make a difference. The creation of a new life for humanity depends upon our willingness to use our new-found power to shake up the status quo of deadness, to bring down the Jericho walls of impregnable and unjust institutions by *stamping our feet with new power.* Old things will fall down only when new power stamps its feet; that is, demands a new order, a replacement of lies with truth.

Our recent historical experience with corporate collapses in America alone is a manifestation of the false foundation of lies upon which major institutions are based. When some brave, newly empowered persons stamp their feet by speaking the truth, even the most imposing institution will totter, then fall down.

The closing image of "Escape" is of newly impassioned and empowered people rejoicing with laughter as institutions which were once thought to be untouchable in their dominance and pride simply wither away in the face of truth. In addition to the militant image of stamping feet and falling walls, we have the image of surprisingly fragile institutions being exposed to the flame of truth and *curling up like burnt paper.*

This poem is Lawrence's vision of what will happen when human beings come into their true wholeness. The vision is expressed in the language of certainty. It is not "if" but "when" we get out of the glass bottles of ego and the cages of personality that the new world of passion and truth will come. There is no "if" about it. It will happen.

The poet is sure that human beings will reach the goal of *cool, unlying life* and thus create a new world of truth and laughter which will be triumphantly real and redemptive. Feel that passion and hope, and take heart.

Reclaiming the Soul

Healing

I am not a mechanism, an assembly of various sections.
And it is not because the mechanism is working wrongly, that
        I am ill.
I am ill because of wounds to the soul, to the deep emotional self,
and the wounds to the soul take a long, long time, only time can
        help
and patience, and a certain difficult repentance,
long, difficult repentance, realization of life's mistake, and the
        freeing oneself
from the endless repetition of the mistake
which mankind at large has chosen to sanctify.

The Scientific Doctor

When I went to the scientific doctor
I realized what a lust there was in him to wreak his so called
science on me
and reduce me to the level of a thing.
So I said: Good morning! and left him.

God And The Holy Ghost

There is no sinning against God, what does God care about sin!
But there is sinning against the Holy Ghost, since the Holy
       Ghost is with us
in the flesh, is part of our consciousness.

The Holy Ghost is the deepest part of our own consciousness
wherein we know ourself for what we are
and know our dependence upon the creative beyond.

So if we go counter to our own deepest consciousness
naturally we destroy the most essential self in us,
and once done, there is no remedy, no salvation for this,
nonentity is our portion.

Humility

Nowadays, to talk of humility is a sin against the Holy Ghost.
It is a sneaking evasion of the responsibility
of our own consciousness.

En Masse

Today, society has sanctified
the sin against the Holy Ghost,
and all are encouraged into the sin
so that all may be lost together, en masse, *the great word of our*
civilization.

D.H. Lawrence was in livid rebellion against all modern efforts to explain human nature in some reductive, simplifying way. The method of doing this that seemed most dominant in his time was the mechanistic one.

The industrial revolution had transformed the world in the 19th century by the invention of machines which could do the work of many men. Huge factories sprung up all over the landscape to house the magnificent machinery which held such promise for the creation of a new order of productive plenty.

It was only a matter of time until the machine began to serve as a paradigm for understanding the human body and its functioning. Human bodies could now be defined as most remarkable and intricate machines whose upkeep and efficiency could be delegated to the medical profession. Doctors began to be looked upon as mechanics whose task it was to fix any breakdown or repair any disorder in the mechanism of the human body.

This new paradigm was anathema to Lawrence, a poet nurtured in the romantic tradition which understood human beings as spiritual in nature and as created not in the mold of the machine, but in the image of the divine. So, it is no wonder he cries out at the beginning of his poem called "Healing."

I am not a mechanism, an assembly of various sections.

This sentence was not spoken as a simple denial but as an adamant exclamation of rebellion. It is Lawrence's declaration of war against all efforts to diminish the greatness of the human being by the reductive paradigm of the machine.

Our poet relates an incident from his personal life in a little poem he entitled "The Scientific Doctor." It is a description of his visceral rejection of dehumanization.

> *When I went to the scientific doctor*
> *I realized what a lust there was in him to wreak his so called*
> *science on me*
> *and reduce me to the level of a thing.*
> *So I said: Good morning! and left him.*

So, at both the personal and cultural levels, Lawrence was pitted against mechanistic science and its deleterious effects on human self-understanding.

Lawrence was not only a romantic in his view of human nature, he was also a modernist. He was one of the early poetic modernists in company with Ezra Pound and T.S. Eliot. That is to say, he was not an idealist but a realist about human behavior. He knew there was a greatness in human beings, but also confessed they were deeply flawed.

The modernist in him admitted the sickness of modern man, but the romantic in him denied the sickness was mechanistic in nature. So the next lines of "Healing" declare:

> *And it is not because the mechanism is working wrongly*
>   *that I am ill.*
> *I am ill because of wounds to the soul, to the deep emotional*
>   *self.*

As soon as he utters the word "soul" and refers to the "deep, emotional self," he separates himself from mechanistic thinkers who would define the human being merely as a biological organism equipped with language.

The human predicament is not that we are working wrongly as a mechanism. The deficiency that afflicts us is not physical, but spiritual. We have been wounded at a level deeper than the biological. The soul, a seat of deep emotional feeling, a throbbing, sensitive center of the self, is where the human problem exists. It is at that level, therefore, it must be solved. The soul cannot be mended by physical methods. It cannot be "fixed" and put back on the assembly line in short order.

This affirmation of a spiritual core is a critical part of Lawrence's anthropology. He believed that a human being is created by the combination of three factors—an egg, a sperm, and the Holy Ghost. There is not only a feminine and a masculine source of a human life, but a divine one as well. He goes way back into ancient imagery and renews the use of the now quaint phrase "The Holy Ghost." It is his way of flaunting a distinctly religious image in the face of modernity.

Lawrence believed in the spiritual dignity of the human being. But he also believed that dignity could be lost when a person goes counter to the deep spiritual core within. There is probably no better expression of Lawrence's spiritual vision than the poem entitled "God and The Holy Ghost."

There is no sinning against God, what does God care about sin!
But there is sinning against the Holy Ghost, since the
          Holy Ghost is with us
in the flesh, is part of our consciousness.

The Holy Ghost is the deepest part of our own consciousness
Wherein we know ourself for what we are
and know our dependence upon the creative beyond.

So if we go counter to our own deepest consciousness
naturally we destroy the most essential self in us,
and once done, there is no remedy, no salvation for this,
nonentity is our portion.

In his most pessimistic moments Lawrence believed that most people were "nonentities", that they had sinned against the Holy Ghost within them and thus no longer had a soul to save. That is, though humans are not "things" they can turn themselves into "things" by denying or going counter to their true spiritual center. Lawrence was a spiritual aristocrat in that he believed only a few people were able to realize the spiritual greatness of their lives.

Despite this pessimism and elitism, he does hold out in his poem "Healing" the possibility of renewal and restoration. Spiritual wounds, deep emotional wounds can eventually be healed. Since they are often inflicted by other people, there is a way through and beyond them. Lawrence, at least in this poem, affirms a positive future for the human being who has been afflicted by the unfeeling, mechanistic world.

As the poem proceeds, it outlines three possible sources for healing the wounded condition. The first source of healing comes from the patience to accept the slowness of the process itself.

> *And the wounds of the soul take a long, long time only*
> *time can help*
> *and patience,*

Lawrence here puts to death all magical thinking about the healing of the soul. There is no instantaneous, charismatic healing. All claims of sudden, mysterious spiritual recovery are lies and cannot be trusted. The wounds of the soul are deep, not shallow, and must be honored as such. Healing must begin at the deepest part of the wound and work its way outward until the whole wound is transformed into a completely knitted newness.

That's why "only time can help, and patience." Resorting impatiently to seeking dubious methods of accelerating the healing process is a radical self-deception that leaves one lost and hopeless. Patience, then, is not only a virtue but an absolutely essential pre-requisite for healing the wounds of the human soul.

The second source of healing is what Lawrence calls

...a certain difficult repentance,
long, difficult repentance, realization of life's mistake...

Repentance is a change of mind and heart about the course of life one has been pursuing. It is a mental and emotional "about face," a turning in the opposite direction from one's present momentum. The English word repentance comes from a Greek word, metanoia. Metanoia was a military term of command. The Greek drill sergeant used the command to direct a column of soldiers going in one direction to do a 180 degree turn.

So Lawrence is saying that healing requires a radical re-orientation of life. Mankind, he believed, is marching in a disastrous direction— away from the life of spirit and soul. This is what he calls "life's mistake," the denial of the Holy Ghost, the abandonment of the idea of a spiritual center as a divine gift to each human being.

Repentance means to quit the direction of mere humanism, the reduction of the human being to smaller proportions in contrast to the industrial mega-structures of the modern world. It means to reclaim the soul, the sense of human greatness which comes of its connection to a spiritual source. Perhaps the goal of repentance is the reclaiming of soulful greatness, as may be best expressed in Lawrence's very brief poem called "Humility,"

> *Nowadays, to talk of humility is a sin against the Holy Ghost.*
> *It is a sneaking evasion of the responsibility*
> *of our own consciousness.*

The third source of healing is now clear. It is in action, positive behavioral change in the direction of reclaiming our true nature.

...and

> *the freeing oneself*
> *from the endless repetition of the mistake*
> *which mankind at large has chosen to sanctify.*

There is no healing of the wounds of the soul unless one has the courage to choose a path which most of mankind ignores, belittles, and shames, namely the path of repentance. Healing is a lonely journey, separating us from the majority of our society who simply don't get that there is a Holy Ghost, let alone a way of sinning against it which destroys the inner secret of our greatness.

True individuality demands that we stand alone with unshakeable faith in our spiritual consciousness, refusing to participate in the "endless repetition of that mistake" which mankind sanctifies as only natural.

Lawrence's poem "En Masse" describes the insidious power of society to take us along with it to the only disaster which ultimately matters, the death of our spiritual consciousness:

> *Today, society has sanctified*
> *the sin against the Holy Ghost,*
> *and all are encouraged into the sin*
> *so that all may be lost together,* en masse, *the great*
> *word of our civilization.*

This marvelous poem "Healing" is not only a cry of rebellion against the materialism of modern life. It is also a full-throated appeal for conversion or re-conversion back to the reclamation of the soul, the special spiritual consciousness that alone sets the human individual qualitatively apart. Thus we transcend the mechanistic and soulless degradation of meaning and true life which is the hallmark of our civilization.

Our task is to hear and believe the voice of the poet and act on it so the world's healing may begin once more.

The Connection with Greatness

Sun Men

Men should group themselves into a new order
of sun-men.
Each one turning his breast straight to the sun of suns
in the centre of all things,
and from his own little inward sun
nodding to the great one.

And receiving from the great one
his strength and his promptings,
and refusing the pettifogging promptings of human
*   weakness.*

And walking each in his own sun-glory
With bright legs and uncringing buttocks.

Democracy

*I am a democrat so far as I love the free sun in men
and an aristocrat in so far as I detest the narrow-gutted,
possessive persons.*

*I love the sun in any man
when I see it between his brows
clear and fearless, even if tiny.*

Aristocracy Of The Sun

*To be an aristocrat of the sun
you don't need one single social inferior to exalt you,
you draw your nobility directly from the sun
let other people be what they may.*

*I am that I am
from the sun,
and people are not my measure.*

*Perhaps, if we started right, all the children could grow up
        sunny, and sun-aristocrats.
We need have no dead people, money slaves, and social worms.*

Human bonding is not just an enjoyable dimension of a civilized
life. It is an essential characteristic of the survival of greatness
in human society. D.H. Lawrence looked around at the kind of
human associations prevalent in the British social and economic
life of his day and found them abominable!

They represented to him "the gentrification of the British people." This development deprived the society of the heroic greatness of men and women as well as their artistic sensitivity, both of which are essential to an enduring and endurable common life.

The image of mankind embodied by the English gentry was one of pre-occupation with money and social rank within the confines of a society limited to Great Britain. That image also included the power and ability to subjugate weaker peoples around the globe through war and colonial control, and to perpetuate the conquest of Empire.

This left Lawrence crying out for a whole new way of connecting with human greatness and of forming a truly creative order of humanity. This powerful cry came forth in his poem, "Sun Men." While this poem is gender specific in its expression, Lawrence was speaking of the renewal of all of human life, regardless of gender.

> *Men should group themselves into a new order*
> *of sun men.*
> *Each one turning his breast straight to the sun of suns*
> *in the centre of all things,*
> *and from his own little inward sun*
> *nodding to the great one.*

This new order must be based on humanity's common connection to a power greater than themselves. The sun was Lawrence's favorite symbol for the mystical presence that inhabits and animates the whole universe. Within the universe there is always a creative presence—best symbolized by the sun. The older religions knew this better than the more recent Judeo-Christian faiths.

The weakness of these historical faiths was that they separated man from nature and his original contact with the divine through that medium. Their focus was rather on human figures such as Moses and Jesus, their laws and teachings, and the historical events surrounding them. Through the influence of these figures, human beings were deprived of a more sensuous symbolism of God provided by nature. They were also separated from a more primal connection between people whose unity around natural symbols was a daily practice in their religious life.

Lawrence learned much about this primal religion and its power to bind humanity together in an energetic order. He learned from living close to the Native Americans of New Mexico. This was his favorite place on earth and he is buried in the midst of a mountain forest near Taos.

The men of the Pueblos would gather in a circle at sunrise to lift up their hearts to the sun. They knew that the sun was not God but that behind the sun was the "first of suns"—and that exposure to that sun of suns made men glad and strong all through the day. In New Mexico, Lawrence came in touch with a vast, old religion preceding god-concepts and ideas, a religion in which there were no gods for all is God.

From that time on he rejected all religious thought forms that have no sensual reality grounded in nature. He grounded his personal religion on natural instinct and what he called "blood-knowledge" rather than on the intellect.

His belief system was that there is a principle in the universe itself, towards which man turns religiously—a life of the universe itself. And the heroic human being is the one who touches and transmits the life of the universe.

The natural human response to the great presence is to turn toward it and open to it, and acknowledge it as of greatest importance. That response is described in the poem "Sun Men."

> *Each one turning his breast straight to the sun of suns*
> *in the centre of all things,*
> *and from his own little inward sun*
> *nodding to the great one.*

Here is the recognition that we human beings have an inner core that is attuned to and can connect directly with the source of all things. Lawrence believed that this core was centered in the human body's mid-section, what we would call the gut. It is not in the mind but in the gut we experience, respond, and assent to the center of the universe.

Lawrence believed that the sun is the soul of the inanimate universe and the quick of the sun is polarized with the solar plexus of mankind. He believed that the only way for people to return to a true relationship with each other was to meet in this common ground---belief in their gut connection with the religious core of the universe.

This belief would create the *new order* in place of the old. When humans ignore that common flame of life within them they become obsessed with mere ideas and the outer world. This renders the very sense of a new order distant and impossible.

Human progress can only be achieved when this new order of common bonding and devotion is founded. Lawrence was convinced that only the renewed empowerment of men and women in this way would move the evolution of the human race forward.

This renewed humanity will come from the influx of strength and guidance from the *great one.* So, the *centre of all things* is not simply a passive recipient of praise and devotion. It is a true source of empowerment and enlightenment which supersedes any other source.

The task of humanity is to *refuse the pettifogging promptings of human weakness*, that is, to turn from merely human sources of knowledge and tend to the flow of inspiration and energy coming from the very core of the living universe. Not yielding to the forces of conformity or making capitulation to the old order, humanity will begin to walk, talk, and behave in new and powerful ways. Their whole bodies will come alive with new energy and boldness.

Humanity will shine as never before as they walk with *bright legs*. They will not cower or cringe with fear because they will possess *uncringing buttocks*! They will become creatures of a new order which Lawrence calls an "aristocracy of the sun."

Lawrence says,

> *I am a democrat so far as I love the free sun in men*
> *and an aristocrat in so far as I detest the narrow-gutted,*
> *possessive persons.*

His poem "Aristocracy of the Sun" envisions what it would mean for a new order of sun-beings to come into existence. Feel the nobility of this future as he says:

> *To be an aristocrat of the sun*
> *you don't need one single social inferior to exalt you,*
> *you draw your nobility directly from the sun*
> *let other people be what they may.*
>
> *I am that I am*
> *from the sun,*
> *and people are not my measure.*
>
> *Perhaps, if we started right, all the children could grow up*
> > *sunny*
> *and sun-aristocrats.*
> *We need have no dead people, money slaves, and social*
> > *worms.*

To Lawrence, the survival of greatness in our human society could indeed be insured by the special kind of human bonding he describes in Sun Men. This quality of new order should not be a threat to anyone except those heavily invested in maintaining the old order of superiority and patriarchal dominance.

The utopian vision dear to Lawrence was this—that from childhood each boy and girl would be taught to believe in their true value and their unique giftedness. To grow up as a "sun-aristocrat" would mean that no child would be measured in relation to any other child.

The kind of vicious social stratification which requires that there always be someone to look down on would not be imposed on growing children. "If we started right" all the children would grow up, not as "commoners" but as "aristocrats", that is, aware of their natural greatness and rejoicing in it. They would also perceive and affirm the nobility of each other so that not one child would be put down, trodden on, or despised.

This vision is, of course, the direct opposite of the order of patriarchy which prevailed in the society in which Lawrence grew up. But he was convinced that the social order could be transformed by a new generation of "sun-aristocrats."

Indeed, patriarchy could and would die away as human beings grouped themselves into a new order of sun-beings, each one bonding in solidarity to all others and leading the next leap ahead in humanity's evolution to greatness.

Respecting the Inner Life

The Heart Of Man

There is the other universe, of the heart of man
that we know nothing of, that we dare not explore.
A strange, grey distance separates
our pale mind still from the pulsing continent
of the heart of man.

Forerunners have barely landed on the shore
and no man knows, no woman knows
the mystery of the interior
when darker still than Congo or Amazon
flow the heart's rivers of fullness, desire, and distress.

Terra Incognita

There are vast realms of consciousness still undreamed of
vast ranges of experience, like the humming of unseen harps,
we know nothing of, within us.
Oh when man has escaped from the barbed wire entanglement
of his own ideas and his own mechanical devices

there is a marvelous rich world of contact and sheer fluid beauty
and fearless face-to-face awareness of now-naked life
and me, and you, and other men and women
and grapes, and ghouls, and ghosts and green moonlight
and ruddy orange limbs stirring the limbo
of the unknown air, and eyes so soft
softer than the space between the stars,
and all things, and nothing, and being and not-being
alternately palpitant,
when at last we escape the barbed-wire enclosure
of "Know Thyself," knowing we can never know,
we can but touch, and wonder, and ponder, and make our effort
and dangle in a last fastidious fine delight
as the fuchsia does, dangling her reckless drop
of purple after so much putting forth
and slow mounting marvel of a little tree.

D.H. Lawrence lived in a time of great psychological exploration. Both Sigmund Freud and Carl Jung had shocked the world of traditional medicine and anthropology, as well as religion and morality, through their revelations about just how little human beings were in conscious control of their behavior.

They had unfolded the disturbing truth of unconscious motivation. They thus had made clear that buried passions of love and hate, fear and desire, were more influential in determining daily life than any conscious aspirations or intentions.

In his poem, "The Heart of Man," Lawrence expressed both the terror and the wonder of facing this whole new land of humanity's unknown depths. He called the interior life "the other universe," that is, a realm of reality distinct from the space-time universe that fills our five senses so overwhelmingly.

There is the other universe, of the heart of man

that we know nothing of, that we dare not explore.
A strange, grey distance separates
our pale mind still from the pulsing continent
of the heart of man.

Actually, all of Lawrence's novels and most of his poems were given to the exploration of the inner life of men and women and of how the unknown parts of their psyches impacted mightily the drama of their relationships to each other.

So, Lawrence himself was a famous explorer, not of uncharted global territory like Columbus or Cortez, Marco Polo or Dr. Livingstone, but of the other universe of inner life and mystery.

By the time Lawrence died in March of 1930 almost every place on the planet earth had been discovered, explored, and mapped. The mysteries of the physical earth were being mastered and explained, and scientifically documented. The great historical era of exploration and discovery that had been such a source of thrilling adventure for previous generations had now come and gone.

It was left to his generation, he believed, to continue the quest of discovery, but now the unknown territory was "the pulsing continent of the heart of man." He admits, at the outset, the difficulty of getting the "pale mind" of man to begin overcoming the "strange grey distance" and actually setting foot on the new territory which was already daunting the early explorers of the heart of humanity. Here is how he expresses the dilemma he felt.

Forerunners have barely landed on the shore
and no man knows, no woman knows
the mystery of the interior
when darker still than Congo or Amazon
flow the heart's rivers of fullness, desire, and distress.

This is a magnificent affirmation of the emotional depths of the human soul. The Congo and the Amazon, the largest rivers yet discovered, each one reaching thousands of miles into the dark interior of their respective lands, are still but inadequate metaphors of the mysteries of the human soul and its passions. Forerunners (read Freud and Jung) have barely established a beachhead in their efforts to plunge into the jungles of human emotional and spiritual complexity.

So the call is clear, the challenge daunting, the romance irresistible as we moderns stand awestruck before the depths and breadths of our own inner worlds. Who knows what discoveries await us? Who can imagine the wonders that lie ahead, or the terrors that lurk in the shadows, or the incredible powers for good or evil that will begin to manifest themselves and dwarf all previous understandings of the moral and spiritual potential of the human race?

Lawrence knew the first step in the adventure ahead was for a human *to escape from the barbed wire entanglement of his own ideas and his own mechanical devices.* The great killer of the adventurous spirit in his time was self-satisfied grandiosity about humanity's present understanding of itself and its vision of the purpose of human life and endeavor.

The industrial revolution had produced a limited view of mankind as primarily a "tool-maker" whose destiny depended upon inventing more and more machinery performing ever more wonderful feats of manufacture to satisfy the lust for an exponential number of external things, leading mankind on to a material paradise unparalleled in human history.

The opposite view, taken by Lawrence and other great writers and poets of the time, was simply that the truly beckoning adventure was to explore the depths of humanity's inwardness, the capacities for beauty, wonder, and imagination. It was to come to know the vast ranges of aesthetic experience and creativity which could turn the world into a pulsing organism of artistic, literary, and spiritual production, astounding humanity with ever-mounting marvel and appreciation.

In his poem, "Terra Incognita," Lawrence affirms this compelling vision by displaying the poetic versatility of imagination which would mark the coming age of inner exploration.

There are vast realms of consciousness still undreamed of
vast ranges of experience, like the humming of unseen harps,
we know nothing of, within us.
Oh when man has escaped from the barbed wire entanglement
of his own ideas and his own mechanical devices
there is a marvelous rich world of contact and sheer fluid beauty
and fearless face-to-face awareness of now-naked life
and me, and you, and other men and women
and grapes, and ghouls, and ghosts and green moonlight
and ruddy orange limbs stirring the limbo
of the unknown air, and eyes so soft
softer than the space between the stars,
and all things, and nothing, and being and not-being
alternately palpitant,
when at last we escape the barbed-wire enclosure
of "Know Thyself," knowing we can never know,
we can but touch, and wonder, and ponder, and make our effort
and dangle in a last fastidious fine delight
as the fuchsia does, dangling her reckless drop
of purple after so much putting forth
and slow mounting marvel of a little tree.

In this great poem of the imagination, Lawrence lets himself go in a paean of praise for the "marvelous rich world of contact and sheer fluid beauty" that awaits any person willing to become an explorer of *the other universe*. He means for his prolific imagination to stir our own imaginal powers into new life.

How do we, in this present time, become explorers of the *pulsing continent of the heart of man?* We begin by simply respecting the inner life of humanity as of supreme importance. We begin by respecting our own individual inner life as the most prolific source of meaning and energy available to us on our human journey.

Our hardest challenge in accomplishing this radical shift of emphasis is to overcome the extraverted prejudice that dominates our modern consciousness. This prejudice declares in a peculiar kind of spiritual blindness that the external world is where the action really is. The world of work and commerce, buying and selling, getting and spending, exercises such a paralyzing fascination for us that we rarely realize that what is going on inside us is infinitely more important than what is going on around us.

The advertising blitz and the media bombardment characteristic of our modern communication world are both designed to convince us that the external events and material goods with which we are surrounded deserve our constant expenditure of time, money, and attention. "Look no further for satisfaction and meaning," they tell us, "this is what it's all about."

Meanwhile, our souls go hungry for the sustenance that only the exploration of the inner world can supply. The heart of humanity grows ever more lonely waiting for the appearance of that adventurous explorer who, in order to feed the emptiness at the center of human life, discovers and describes the wonders of *the other universe.* The need was never greater for some aesthetic adventurers to renounce the comfort zone of external things and turn their attention, and ours, to the true marvels hidden in the inner life of the human race.

Respecting the inner life means beginning with ourselves. How do we do that? Some probing questions are in order. What is our heart's deepest desire? What rivers of fullness and distress flow through us? What is our true calling in life? Do we ever express what is deepest within us through writing, journaling, painting, composing, sculpting, or creating any work of art that expresses who we are? Do we read works that unfold the inner life of human beings in a classic and unforgettable way? Or, do we, at least, collect, appreciate, and share these works in a way that blesses others?

These are not idle questions which we can ignore without fear of consequences. The very quality of our existence depends on our commitment to respect our inner life and honor it by giving it whatever creative expression its nature demands. True, we can never plumb the entire depths even of our own individual creativity. As Lawrence has it, *we can but touch, and wonder, and ponder, and make our effort.* Yet, everything that is truly human in us cries out for that effort to be made.

If you are looking for a fellow-adventurer to take the journey with you into the deep places of the universe of human wonder and greatness, could you do any better than to take D.H. Lawrence and seek his help in awakening the very center of your soul to all the glory that shines from the darkness and beckons to us even now? His novels and poems unfold our human depths in a way rarely equaled in modern literature.

The fact that he left this earth physically over seventy-five years ago does not prevent his opening our hearts today to the kind of appreciative consciousness it requires to value above all else the *other universe* of the inner life of humanity, including especially, our own.

The Power of Authentic Feeling

Cerebral Emotions

I am sick of people's cerebral emotions
that are born in their minds and forced down by the will
on to their poor, deranged bodies.

People feeling things they intend to feel, they mean to feel,
they will feel,
just because they don't feel them.

For, of course, if you really feel something
you don't have to assert that you feel it.

Blank

At present I am a blank, and I admit it.
In feeling I am just a blank.
My mind is fairly nimble, and is not blank.

*My body likes its dinner, and the warm sun, but otherwise is
blank.*

*My soul is almost blank, my spirits quite.
I have a certain amount of money, so my anxieties are blank.*

*And I can't do anything about it, even there I am blank.
So I am just going to go on being a blank, till something nudges
    me from within,
and makes me know I am not blank any longer.*

To Women, As Far As I'm Concerned

*The feelings I don't have I don't have.
The feelings I don't have, I won't say I have.
The feelings you say you have, you don't have.
The feelings you would like us both to have, we neither of
        us have.*

*The feelings people ought to have, they never have.
If people say they've got feelings, you may be pretty
        sure they haven't got them.*

*So if you want either of us to feel anything at all
you'd better abandon all ideas of feelings altogether.*

Human beings sometimes made D.H. Lawrence sick. They did
so by being pretentious about their feelings. People were smart
enough to know what they ought to be feeling, so they would make
up a story about how strongly or sweetly they felt and then would
seek to convince others of what "feeling" persons they were. In

other words, they lied, both to themselves and to others, about what and even how much they were feeling.

This lack of authenticity in the life of the feelings nauseated Lawrence almost beyond words, but not entirely. In an occasional poem he blurted out his own truth about the sickness he felt:

> *I am sick of people's cerebral emotions*
> *that are born in their minds and forced down by the will*
> *on to their poor deranged bodies.*
>
> *People feeling things they intend to feel, they mean to feel,*
> *they* will *feel,*
> *just because they don't feel them.*
>
> *For, of course, if you really feel something*
> *you don't have to assert that you feel it.*

Authentic feeling, Lawrence knew, originates in the body, not the mind. It is a matter of instinct and intuition, and stirs first of all in what he called the plexuses and ganglia of the nervous system. If a human being tries to design or manufacture a feeling-response to an external situation of demand, distress, or social expectation, deep down he/she will know it is a lie rather than the truth, and therefore it will create distance from others, not closer bonding.

Waiting for true feelings to emerge from the psycho/physical depths is the hardest challenge we humans face in the complex array of social contacts and situations. The temptation is to use our cleverness to summon an expression of feeling because we know it is either expected or hoped for by others. To succumb to this temptation, according to Lawrence, is to spread death, not life, throughout our human contacts.

The image of the English gentleman, always expressing the "appropriate" feeling, always saying the "right" thing, always calibrating his actions, not to his own true feelings, but to the exigencies of the social moment, was completely anathema to D.H. Lawrence. The passion in his poetry and in his novels is meant to displace this image of the English gentleman with a more earthy, body-grounded kind of feeling human being.

He cried out for a new humanity based on the blood, the bone, and the genitals. He begged for humans to trust their instincts, their bodily intuition, and their more primitive sensibilities about how they felt in any given situation, and thus reclaim their lost authenticity in the realm of feelings. He wanted them to speak of their feelings only when they rose up from the depths of their nervous system, or else keep silent and be honest.

If no feelings appear or are present in the moment, a person should admit it and live with that truth of emptiness until something changes. In his poem entitled simply, "Blank," Lawrence models the honest confession about the non-feeling or pre-feeling state:

At present I am a blank, and I admit it.
In feeling I am just a blank.
My mind is fairly nimble, and is not blank.
My body likes its dinner, and the warm sun, but otherwise is blank.
My soul is almost blank, my spirit quite.
I have a certain amount of money, so my anxieties are blank.
And I can't do anything about it, even there I am blank.
So I am just going to go on being a blank, till something nudges me
*   from within,*
and makes me know I am not blank any longer.

This poem is Lawrence's great affirmation of honesty in one's feelings. His way was to manufacture no feeling, no matter how dead his emotional life was at a given time. He knew sometimes simple waiting was the only true path to authenticity. Waiting for what? Waiting *till something nudges me from within, and makes me know I am not a blank any longer.* He is no longer blank when a deep visceral stirring tells him a powerful new life-force in the form of a feeling is about to resurrect his deadened senses and set him in the midst of the garden of renewed emotional connection.

Waiting for the depths of the soul to stir into life again is made harder by the world around one. The present world is so "outer-directed" through social pressures and advertising lures, people rarely get to experience the subtle movements of "inner-directedness." The question, "What is the next right step for me?" does not receive much time or attention. A full calendar beguiles us from tending an empty soul. The outer agenda pre-empts our mental space to such a degree that the inner agenda is simply forgotten.

To become conscious of the blankness of the soul and of the need to wait for its next movements or emergence is what saves us from the soul-less busyness that characterizes our days.

If we cannot wait, we will sooner or later force ourselves to feel something, and that will land us in a dangerous, threatening situation where our true center of feeling will be in jeopardy of extinction. Lawrence was opposed to all those teachers in the course of history who gave forceful commandments or passionate advice about what, ideally, we ought to feel. Even if they were telling us that we ought to love our fellow men or that we ought to have sympathy for the weak and downtrodden of earth, we must resist any action on these *principles* if the deepest core of feeling in us is not stirring in that direction on its own volition and momentum.

This truth will be clearer as you read Lawrence's two couplets, "Retort To Jesus" and "Retort To Whitman." These two great teachers made urgent appeals to human beings to love and show sympathy for others and that this is the way we "ought to feel and act." So Lawrence replies,

Retort To Jesus

And whoever forces himself to love anybody
begets a murderer in his own body.

Retort To Whitman

And whoever walks a mile full of false sympathy
walks to the funeral of the whole human race.

This harsh rejection of the compassionate advice of two of history's greatest teachers gives a clear idea of how rabidly protective Lawrence was of emotional authenticity.

It was in his relationship with women that Lawrence found his devotion to emotional authenticity tested in the extreme. Women who were freely expressive of their feelings toward him expected, of course, a direct reciprocation of some kind. This situation became so uncomfortable for him at times that he said in one of his short poems, "Can't Be Borne,"

> *Any woman who says to me*
> *—Do you really love me? —*
> *earns my undying detestation.*

Though Lawrence is sometimes called a misogynist due to remarks like these, he had several deep and meaningful relationships with women before he met the one true love of his life, Frieda Weekly, the wife of the Department Head of the University at which

Lawrence was a beginning professor. Frieda and Lawrence had such an immediate visceral connection to each other that they went to bed and made love within twenty minutes of their first meeting. It was from his passionate connection with Frieda, before and after their marriage and right up until his untimely death from tuberculosis at 44 years of age, that Lawrence derived his deepest experiences of authentic feeling.

His wisdom from that experience was what he put into his poetry about male/female relationships and in his novels which are virtually all about the challenging struggle of men and women to find that wonderful place of genuine feeling for each other.

One of Lawrence's best known poems contains lines of brutal honesty about the feeling situation between a man and a woman. It is a poem of rebellion against being coerced by too much talk about feelings in a couple's budding relationship.

This poem is a powerful tonic for a lack of authenticity in relationships, a tonic which, if administered early enough, can clear out the unreal romantic expression in a growing relationship and give the couple an opportunity to reframe their connection in an honest, open way. This poem is titled "To Women, As Far As I'm Concerned."

> *The feelings I don't have I don't have.*
> *The feelings I don't have, I won't say I have.*
> *The feelings you say you have, you don't have.*
> *The feelings you would like us both to have, we*
> *   neither of us have.*
> *The feelings people ought to have, they never have.*
> *If people say they've got feelings, you may be pretty*
> *   sure they haven't got them.*
>
> *So if you want either of us to feel anything at all*
> *you'd better abandon all ideas of feelings altogether.*

The one great truth we can learn here and almost everywhere in D.H. Lawrence's work, a truth that would deepen and strengthen our human connection with each other, regardless of gender, is that pretentiousness about our feelings for each other creates an eventual certainty of shipwreck in our efforts to create a lasting bond of love or friendship.

Honesty, especially in matters of the heart, is not only the best policy, but the only saving grace making it possible for us to share successfully the long-term human journey together.

Restoring the Natural Greatness of Humanity

Lizard

A lizard ran out on a rock and looked up, listening
no doubt to the sounding of the spheres.
And what a dandy fellow! the right toss of a chin for you
and swirl of a tail!

If men were as much men as lizards are lizards
they'd be worth looking at.

A Man

All I care about in a man
is that unbroken spark in him
where he is himself
undauntedly.

And all I want is to see the spark flicker
vivid and clean.

But our civilization, alas,
with lust crushes out the spark
and leaves men living clay.

Because when the spark is crushed in a man
he can't help being a slave, a wage-slave,
a money-slave.

Fatigue

My soul has had a long, hard day
she is tired,
she is seeking her oblivion.

O, and in the world
there is no place for the soul to find her oblivion,
the after darkness of her peace,
for man has killed the silence of the earth
and ravished all the peaceful oblivious places
where the angels used to alight.

D.H. Lawrence had a deep, abiding love of nature and its creatures. Many of his poems were about individual insects and animals, their character and their characteristics. He wrote, for example, about the mosquito, the bat, the fish, and in one of his most renowned pieces about the snake. In these nature poems, he imagined the human qualities of these creatures and sought to penetrate to the soul-level of the animal and discern something of its inner life.

He was particularly impressed with the beauty and dignity of the lizard, a creature often shunned and despised by human beings. During his stays in Mexico and the American southwest he had often seen the grand appearance of an iguana climbing upon an elevated pile of rock and striking a long, silent pose worthy of the best nature-photography.

In his poem entitled simply "Lizard" he pictures the very moment when this creature attains a position of maximum display and seems in touch with both a higher order of reality and his own natural magnificence:

> *A lizard ran out on a rock and looked up, listening*
> *no doubt to the sounding of the spheres.*
> *And what a dandy fellow! the right toss of a chin for you*
> *and swirl of a tail!*
>
> *If men were as much men as lizards are lizards*
> *they'd be worth looking at.*

The wistful little couplet at the close of this poem reveals Lawrence's great disappointment in modern people. He perceives that human beings were intended to display the same quality of magnificence in bearing, the same sensitivity to the *sounding of the spheres*, the same obvious and admirable grandiosity as the lizard. They were intended to manifest their beauty as a natural gift from the creator, as their natural inheritance from nature itself. But alas, modern people, including men were, as a whole, not worth looking at.

Human greatness was to be a natural growth from within, uninterrupted by false ideals or images of what humans ought to be. The substitution of any kind of platonic ideal or cultural norm by which humanity is defined is a sin against nature's original intention. The rejection of all such substitutes is an essential step in restoring the natural greatness of human beings.

In our own day, many have little concept of what the phrase "the natural greatness of humanity" might mean. This is a clear sign that an inner search for what is missing must take place. How shall they proceed to discover their lost greatness?

Lawrence believed that people were endowed with a "blood-consciousness," a dark, instinctive, intuitive mode of knowing by which they could perceive who they were to become. This was superior to the "brain-consciousness" which was a kind of intellectual awareness easily influenced by external factors and social pressures. As Lawrence put it, "You can idealize or intellectualize, or you can let the dark soul in you see for itself."

When people learn to trust this deeper knowing about their own nature and allow it to manifest in their bearing and behavior, then they will be *worth looking at.* Their natural beauty will shine forth with a new brilliance and they will no longer be discounted as having fallen short of the expectations and demands of their society. The powerful, mystical sense of their own greatness will bring a calm, centered self-confidence into their lives and they will begin to embody the grandeur they were born to bear.

Obviously, the modern world has created barriers to this deeper self-realization. Civilization itself militates against humanity's natural greatness.

One of the ways this happens is made clear in Lawrence's poem, "A Man."

> *All I care about in a man*
> *is that unbroken spark in him*
> *where he is himself*
> *undauntedly.*
>
> *And all I want is to see the spark flicker*
> *vivid and clean.*

But our civilization, alas,
with lust crushes out the spark
and leaves men living clay.

Because when the spark is crushed in a man
he can't help being a slave, a wage-slave,
a money-slave.

The demands of a competitive system are a huge burden which crush the spark of natural greatness. Human beings cease living out of their natural core of self-appreciation and become slaves to a system where the overwhelming message is, "Get money or eat dirt."

They are judged then not by their intrinsic value, but by their market value. The competitive system becomes a giant bully that pushes everyone around so that they can no longer be themselves, but they:

> *are forced to do a thousand mean things meaner than*
> > *your nature,*
> *and forced to clutch onto possessions in the hope they'll*
> > *make you feel safe,*
> *and forced to watch everyone that comes near you, lest*
> > *they've come to do you down.* ("Being Alive")

So, maintaining natural greatness requires that we find some way to deal with this system of competitive self-centeredness. A revolution could overthrow the system, but that is clearly a task that requires more than a single lifetime of effort.

In the meantime, two values must guide those who would survive the system and continue to manifest natural greatness.

One of the values is trust. *Without a bit of common trust in one another, we can't live. In the end, we go insane.* So, says Lawrence, few people you can trust and bond with them as though your life depended on it, for indeed, it does."

Why is trust so essential to the manifestation of human greatness? Simply because only in an atmosphere of trust does a person feel safe. Human beings will not bring forth the elements of their greatness if it is deemed unsafe to do so. They must be surrounded by a community of others who believe in their greatness and who encourage them to express it in whatever way is natural for them.

The truth is we are afraid of our own greatness. This fear can only be assuaged by a supportive community whose trust provides a safe container in which our full potential is welcomed into bold expression.

The second value is generosity. This is the opposite of competitive selfishness. *To be alive, you've got to feel a generous flow—the world is waiting for a great new movement of generosity or for a great wave of death.*

Human greatness withers if it is withheld. Generosity is the opposite of withholding. It is a pouring out, indeed a gushing forth, of the gifts a human individual possesses. These gifts grow deeper and stronger as they are shared with others.

The surest way to destroy a person's belief in their own greatness is to convince them their talent is not worth sharing. Stifling the outward flow of creative self-giving is the way to bring the "great wave of death" Lawrence spoke of so chillingly.

The natural greatness of humanity will be restored by a return to a life-style marked by generosity of self-giving and creative self-expression. The greatness is already present, nascent in the human psyche, ready to break forth in awesome beauty and power.

All that is needed is for men and women to break through the timid, shame-based withholding of their truth and beauty. Then they can proceed with unprecedented boldness to become the generous, out-pouring givers of all the good gifts with which they are endowed. This alone will break the magic spell cast on humanity by the competitive system of "get while the getting's good," and bring in a new day of liberated generosity.

Another way in which modern life works against the maintenance of natural greatness is in its crushing of opportunities for rest and spiritual recovery. The world's busyness has left little room for sacred time and sacred space for the restoration of the soul. Lawrence makes this powerfully clear in his poem "Fatigue."

> *My soul has had a long, hard day*
> *she is tired,*
> *she is seeking her oblivion.*
>
> *O, and in the world*
> *there is no place for the soul to find her oblivion,*
>
> *for man has killed the silence of the earth*
> *and ravished all the peaceful oblivious places*
> *where the angels used to alight.*

The need of the human soul for silence and solitude has been clearly voiced by great men who knew that need in their own experience. A renowned British philosopher once said that a man's religion is what he does with his solitariness, and if he is never solitary, he is rarely religious.

The psalmist spoke a similar truth when he penned the now famous words: *Be still, and know that I am God.* So many of our doubts about the reality of a higher power and our own connection to that power come from the fact that we refuse to sit in silence in a room, waiting for the deeper awareness of the divine reality.

Each person who would reclaim his/her natural greatness must return to their mystical intuition and their *blood knowledge* of what it is to be a human being in the fullness of glory. Then he/she must outsmart the slavish money system by cultivating the spirit of ego-less generosity. And, in addition, seek out those few human beings who can be truly trusted and bind them close with "hoops of steel." And, above all, seek out those silent, sacred spaces where *the angels alight*, that is, where the presence of the spirit abides and feeds the human soul. The ability to do these things must be inspired and empowered by the realization that the whole human enterprise on earth hangs in the balance.

Passionate Living

The Primal Passions

*If you will go down into yourself, under your surface personality
you will find you have a great desire to drink life direct
from the source, not out of bottles and bottled personal vessels.*

*What the old people call immediate contact with God.
That strange essential communication of life
not bottled in human bottles.*

*What even the wild witchcraft of the past was seeking
before it degenerated.*

*Life from the source, unadulterated
with the human taint.*

*Contact with the sun of suns
that shines somewhere in the atom, somewhere pivots the
          curved space,
and cares not a straw for the put-up human figments.*

*Communion with the Godhead, they used to say in the past.
But even that is human-tainted now,
tainted with the ego and the personality.*

To feel a fine, fine breeze blowing through the navel and
      the knees
and have a cool sense of truth, inhuman truth at last
softly fluttering the senses, in the exquisite orgasm of coition
with the Godhead of energy that cannot tell lies.

The cool, cool truth of pure vitality
pouring into the veins from the direct contact with the source.
Uncontaminated by even the beginnings of a lie.
The soul's first passion is for sheer life
entering in shocks of truth, unfouled by lies.

And the soul's next passion is to reflect
and then turn round and embrace the extant body of life
with the thrusting embrace of new justice, new justice
between men and men, men and women, and earth and
      stars and suns.
The passion of justice being profound and subtle
and changing in a flow as all passions change.

But the passion of justice is a primal embrace
between man and all his known universe.

And the passion of truth is the embrace between man and
      his god
in the sheer coition of the life-flow, stark and unlying.

Climb Down, O Lordly Mind

...
The blood knows in darkness, and forever dark,
in touch, by intuition, instinctively.
The blood also knows religiously,

and of this the mind is incapable,
The mind is non-religious.

...

Only that exists which exists in my consciousness
Cogito, ergo sum.
Only that exists which exists dynamically and unmentalized
 in my blood.
Non cogito, ergo sum,
I am, I do not think I am.

It was Socrates who said, "The unexamined life is not worth living." It was D.H. Lawrence who could have said, "The un-impassioned life is not worth living." He was convinced that every human being had a buried passion deep within. Finding and living this passion was the only path to a truly human life. This passion was not manufactured by humans, but given to them as a gift of the universe. The ongoing challenge to every person is to go and find the treasure buried within them. Thus the poem, "The Primal Passions."

> *If you will go down into yourself, under your surface*
> > *personality*
> *you will find you have a great desire to drink life direct*
> *from the source, not out of bottles and bottled personal*
> > *vessels.*
>
> *What the old people call immediate contact with God.*
> *That strange essential communication of life*
> *not bottled in human bottles.*
>
> *What even the wild witchcraft of the past was seeking*
> *before it degenerated.*
>
> *Life from the source, unadulterated*
> *with the human taint.*

The first word of this poem is the key one—"If". The discovery of life's deepest passion is a choice, a decision one makes. The passion is indeed a gift, but the discovery of it is not, but rather requires a profound effort of will. It is an open question whether any person will have the courage to *go down into yourself.* Lawrence was really pessimistic about the bulk of humanity ever finding their *great desire to drink life direct from the source.*

In spite of a world's literature full of inspiration, urging human beings to seek the source, the hearts of most seemed to Lawrence impervious to the challenge.

The psalmist, for example, exclaimed:

> *As the hart panteth after the waterbrooks*
> *So panteth my soul after thee, O God.*
> *My soul longeth, yea thirsteth for the Living God.* (Psalm 42:1)

Most human beings rather preferred to drink life, not direct from the source but second-hand, *bottled in human bottles.* As a matter of fact, Lawrence viewed most religious organizations as *bottling companies.* They didn't point people directly to the source for an *immediate contact with God,* but rather served up a limited amount carefully prepared and dispensed in bottles. That way, neither they nor their devotees could get carried away into the awesomeness of *that strange essential communication of life, life from the source, unadulterated with the human taint.*

Lawrence believed this experience of contact with God needed no human mediation, but was available to each human being by virtue of his being imbedded in nature itself. Nature, in both its macrocosmic and microcosmic forms carried the potential for immediate revelation. He describes it:

Contact with the sun of suns
that shines somewhere in the atom, somewhere pivots the
curved space,
and cares not a straw for the put-up human figments.

Communion with the Godhead, they used to say in the
past.
But even that is human-tainted now,
tainted with the ego and the personality.

So, the desire to *drink life direct from the source* can have its satisfaction through the contact of our human bodies with the ever—available energy of the universe, whether that energy is seen as in the sun, or the atom, or in that energy beyond observable space called by Lawrence the "sun of suns," that is, not the energy of the actual sun, but the energy that lies behind all the suns, all the concrete manifestations of heavenly bodies.

But, he says, if you try to name this magnificent creative energy by calling it even *the Godhead,* you have gone too far, over-stepped your humanity, asserted your ego, inserted your personality into a sphere that needs no human taint.

Well then, how do we apprehend this ever-present energy and *drink life direct from the source?* Lawrence was convinced that it was through the medium of the human body, not the mind. He believed that the body was a marvelous sensorium which could be a vibrating, pulsing container capable of feeling the source-energy of the universe and also having intercourse with it.

How else can one understand this next passage of "The Primal Passions":

To feel a fine, fine breeze blowing through the navel
and the knees
and have a cool sense of truth, inhuman truth at last

> *softly fluttering the senses, in the exquisite orgasm of*
> > *coition*
> > *with the Godhead of energy that cannot tell lies.*
>
> *The cool, cool truth of pure vitality*
> *pouring into the veins from the direct contact with the*
> > *source.*
> *Uncontaminated by even the beginnings of a lie.*

It was hard for Lawrence's contemporaries to grasp his emphasis on the body as a sensorium of the divine. This was so especially when he got specific and claimed that the human soul is not located in the mind, a la Rene Descartes, but was rather located in the solar plexus, the major ganglia of the nervous system, and in the coursing of the blood.

His conviction was that we know the reality of the divine in these places first and fundamentally, and only then does the mind step in and make up a story that claims to be the truth, and is really a cerebral lie. In the poem of Lawrence's called "Climb Down, O Lordly Mind," he says, for example:

> *The blood knows in darkness, and forever dark,*
> *in touch, by intuition, instinctively.*
> *The blood also knows religiously,*
> *and of this the mind is incapable,*
> *The mind is non-religious.*

Then Lawrence poses the contrast between Descartes' mental knowing and his own bodily knowing:

> *Only that exists which exists in my consciousness*
> *Cogito, ergo sum.*
> *Only that exists which exists dynamically,*
> > *unmentalised, in my blood.*
> *Non cogito, ergo sum,*
> *I am, I do not think I am.*

The next section of "The Primal Passions" makes clear that the *great desire to drink life direct from the source* opens the whole body to experience and display two other passions. One is the passion for truth which is the desire to rid life of its contamination by lies. The other is the passion for justice which embraces:

> *the extant body of life*
> *with the thrusting embrace of new justice*
> *between men and men, men and women, and earth and*
> *stars and suns.*
> *between man and all his known universe.*

As these new passions arrive, they will bring an end to the dullness and machine-like quality of human living. Instead of the distracting, extraverted state of mind focused on things, people will *go down into themselves, under their surface personalities.* There they will find a wondrous, thrilling order of reality, more fascinating by far than anything to be found in the outer world of men and machines and money.

They will discover new energies motivating their lives and relationships. The passion for truth will make them restless with the false facades that most human beings put up to conceal the real truth of who they are, and this dissatisfaction will make creative havoc as they insist on speaking the truth of what they see and feel.

Also, the passion for justice will make them angry with the prejudice and discrimination that divides human beings into competing and self-defeating separateness. They will be unable to rest content with the status quo of gender stratification and the destructive neglect of ecology.

But, that original "if" at the beginning of the poem still hangs in the air as a challenge to human complacency and shallowness. The drama of human life is marked by the presence of that awesome possibility of choosing to go *down and in* to explore what Lawrence called "that other universe of the heart and soul of man." The fate of humanity in our time will be determined by what contemporary human beings decide.

Mankind's True Vocation

We Are Transmitters

As we live, we are transmitters of life.
And when we fail to transmit life, life fails to flow through us.

That is part of the mystery of sex, it is a flow onwards.
Sexless people transmit nothing.

And if, as we work, we can transmit life into our work,
life, still more life, rushes into us to compensate, to be ready
and we ripple with life through the days.

Even if it is a woman making an apple dumpling, or a man
          a stool
if life goes into the pudding, good is the pudding
good is the stool,
content is the woman, with fresh life rippling into her,
content is the man.

Give and it shall be given unto you
is still the truth about life.
But giving life is not so easy.
It doesn't mean handing it out to some mean fool, or letting
          the living dead eat you up.
It means kindling the life-quality where it was not,
even if it's only in the whiteness of a washed pocket
handkerchief.

Work

There is no point in work
unless it absorbs you
like an absorbing game.

If it doesn't absorb you
if it's never any fun,
don't do it.

When a man goes out into his work
he is alive like a tree in spring,
he is living, not merely working.

All That We Have Is Life

All that we have, while we live, is life;
and if you don't live during your life, you are a piece of dung.
And work is life, and life is lived in work
unless you're a wage-slave.
While a wage-slave works, he leaves life aside
and stands there a piece of dung.

Men should refuse to be lifelessly at work.
Men should refuse to be heaps of wage-earning dung.
Men should refuse to work at all, as wage-slaves.
Men should demand to work for themselves, of themselves,
        and put their life in it.
For if a man has no life in his work, he is mostly a heap of dung.

O! Start A Revolution

O! start a revolution, somebody!
not to get the money
but to lose it for ever.

O! start a revolution, somebody!
not to install the working classes
but to abolish the working classes for ever
and have a world of men.

D.H. Lawrence once made the surprising remark that he had never worked a day in his life. How could this be? How could one of the most prolific of authors say such a thing? He produced more novels, poems, articles and letters in his short forty-four year life-span than most have done in a much longer life. It can only be because his vision of work differed in some profound way from that of other writers and poets. If this is so, it is worth a deeper exploration.

One of the fundamental questions of life is a vocational one. What is my work? Do I have a calling that is uniquely mine to pursue? Or am I just here to make money so I can pay for the costs of my existence and not burden my progeny with a load of unpaid debt?

Lawrence gained his own clarity about this issue by making a distinction between two kinds of work. The deadly kind of work was to be a *wage-slave* or a *money-slave*, that is, to join the machine-dominated culture of the so-called industrial age and spend the rest of your life as *a monkey minding a machine*.

On the other hand, the life-giving kind of work is a vocation in which one can pour oneself out in creative self-donation, and in which one is a conduit for the continuous flow of genuine life-generating feeling.

In the poem, "We Are Transmitters" he describes mankind's true vocation:

> *As we live, we are transmitters of life.*
> *And when we fail to transmit life, life fails to flow*
> > *through us.*
>
> *That is part of the mystery of sex; it is a flow onwards*
> *Sexless people transmit nothing.*
>
> *And if, as we work, we can transmit life into our work,*
> *life, still more life, rushes into us to compensate, to be*
> > *ready*
> > *and we ripple with life through the days.*

In other words, creative work is a mysterious flow of energy, even erotic energy, from oneself into the article or the service being produced for the benefit of others. Only when we consent to transmit the flow of energy, do we receive more life from a source beyond ourselves which alone makes further creativity possible.

This is the *ripple* effect which, if we are open to it, will carry us beyond the normal work-a-day world and bless us with true creativity to the end of our days.

The source of human good is this commitment of men and women to being transmitters of life. The humble activities of the kitchen or the workshop can produce a surplus of good for humankind if this flux of life-giving energy is animating them. Here is how Lawrence makes this thought more concrete:

> *Even if it is a woman making an apple dumpling, or a man*
> > *a stool,*
> *if life goes into the pudding, good is the pudding,*

good is the stool,
content is the woman, with fresh life rippling in to her,
content is the man.

It is possible to be content in your work, says Lawrence, when and if you let life ripple into and through you while you are doing it. Your work is twice-blessed. It blesses the person for whom it is done, and blesses the doer of the work with a fresh flow of creative juices for more work.

However, Lawrence issues a warning about the dangers of living the life of self-giving energy.

Give and it shall be given unto you
is still the truth about life.
But giving life is not so easy.
It doesn't mean handing it out to some mean fool, or
letting the living dead eat you up.
It means kindling the life-quality where it was not,
even if it's only in the whiteness of a washed pocket
handkerchief.

The essential truth of this verse is that the self-giving, creative person is not to go unconsciously through life letting him or herself be taken advantage of. There are vampiric people who live off the life blood of creative self-givers. Lawrence wants us to be alert to the truth of exploitation and abuse.

One wonders how many creative life-giving, life-serving people have been drained to the level of complete burn-out by those who take and take and never do otherwise. "Look out for the zombies!" cries Lawrence, the living dead who can only survive by consuming all the good that the creative ones can produce.

Every man and woman must do a regular inventory as to whether his or her energy flow is feeding life or being co-opted by death. One sure way to tell is to ask yourself whether you are feeling energized or drained in this or that situation of self-donation. Do you experience a flow of energy coming into you, kindling new ideas and imaginations? As you *kindle the life-quality where it was not,* do you sense your own life-quality increasing or diminishing?

The clue to look for is if you are conscious of fresh life rippling into you as you spend energy in creative endeavor. If you miss this telltale clue and fail to be aware that replenishment is not happening, your destiny is to become a mere wage-slave or money-slave whose justification for further output is, "Well, you know, I can use the money."

Lawrence gives us further help in testing whether we have lost the livingness in our creative work. A poem entitled simply "Work" asks the crucial question—Has the fun gone out of it for you? He puts it this way:

> *There is no point in work*
> *unless it absorbs you*
> *like an absorbing game.*
>
> *If it doesn't absorb you*
> *if it's never any fun*
> *don't do it.*
>
> *When a man goes out into his work*
> *he is alive like a tree in spring,*
> *he is living, not merely working.*

A tree in spring, of course, is blossoming, bursting forth with the promise of much fruit to come. Does that describe you? Does it come close, at least, or is the tree dead or dying, having had its trunk banded round by those whose greed or envy has driven them to do you to death as a creative human being?

Lawrence is so concerned to have human beings stay alive all their days that he resorts to name-calling in one of his poems just to wake people up. "All That We Have Is Life" is his eager effort to keep everyone alive and flowing with creative energy that he has no nicer name than "dung" for those who fail as transmitters of life.

All that we have, while we live, is life;
and if you don't live during your life, you are a piece of
       dung.
And work is life, and life is lived in work
unless you're a wage-slave.
While a wage-slave works, he leaves life aside
and stands there a piece of dung.

Men should refuse to be lifelessly at work.
Men should refuse to be heaps of wage-earning dung.
Men should refuse to work at all, as wage-slaves.
Men should demand to work for themselves, of themselves,
       and put their life in it.
For if a man has no life in his work, he is mostly a heap
       of dung.

Unfortunately, this poem describes many men and women in our world whose need is to become awake to the waste of time, energy, and yes, soul that characterizes their work life. In the western world especially, men and women in this predicament are described as being in a mid-life crisis. The crisis is simply that unless one can find a place to work and a way of working where one can be alive with the creative flow, can be free of the deadness of more repetitious wage-earning exhaustion, life itself will turn to death, and ongoing despair will be the only destiny left.

Is it any wonder that Lawrence shouts out in one poem

O! start a revolution, somebody!

not to get the money
but to lose it for ever.

O! start a revolution, somebody!
not to install the working classes

but to abolish the working classes for ever
and have a world of men.

Whenever men and women decide deep in the heart to shake off the shackles of meaningless work and find their true vocation, they have started the revolution! They have put their stake in the ground. They have nailed their theses to the door. They have fired the shot heard round the world. They have purely and simply *refused to be lifelessly at work* and have demanded to *work for themselves, of themselves, and put their life into it.*

This is true heroism, true manliness, true womanliness, and to achieve it is both costly and fearful. But when one realizes that he or she has only one chance at life and that it will either be gloriously fulfilled or ignominiously wasted, one dare not hesitate to be a transmitter of life and let life flow through and beyond one for the blessing of the world.

Images of Evil

When Satan Fell

When Satan fell, he only fell
because the Lord Almighty rose a bit too high,
a bit beyond himself.

So Satan only fell to keep a balance.
"Are you so lofty, O my God?
Are you so pure and lofty, up aloft?
Then I will fall, and plant the paths to hell
with vines and poppies and fig trees
so that lost souls may eat grapes
and the moist fig
and put scarlet buds in their hair on the way to hell,
on the way to dark perdition."

And heaven and hell are the scales of the balance of life
which swing against each other.

What Then Is Evil?

Oh, in the world of the flesh of man
iron gives the deadly wound
and the wheel starts the principle of evil.

Oh, in the world of things
the wheel is the first principle of evil.

But in the world of the soul of man
there, and there alone lies the pivot of pure evil
only in the soul of man, when it pivots upon the ego.

When the mind of man makes a wheel which turns on the
        hub of the ego
and the will, the living dynamo, gives the motion and the speed
and the wheel of the conscious self spins on in absolution, absolute
absolute, absolved from the sun and the earth and the moon,
absolute consciousness, absolved from strife and kisses
absolute self-awareness, absolved from the meddling of creation
absolute freedom, absolved from the great necessities of being
then we see evil, pure evil
and we see it only in man
and in his machines.

The Wandering Cosmos

Oh, do not tell me the heavens as well are a wheel.
For every revolution of the earth around the sun
is a footstep onwards, onwards, we know not whither
and we do not care,
but a step onwards in untravelled space,

for the earth, like the sun, is a wanderer.
Their going round each time is a step
onwards, we know not whither,
but onwards, onwards, for the heavens are wandering
the moon and the earth, the sun, Saturn and Betelgeuse,
Vega and Sirius and Altair,
they wander their strange and different ways in heaven
past Venus and Uranus and the signs.

For life is a wandering, we know not whither, but going.

Only the wheel goes round, but it never wanders.
It stays on its hub.

Departure

Now some men must get up and depart
from evil, or all is lost.

...
Evil is upon us and has got hold of us.
Men must depart from it, or all is lost.
We must make an isle impregnable
against evil.

The first truth about evil which D.H. Lawrence asserts is that it is not cosmic in proportion. He rejects the Christian view of history and human life as a cosmic struggle between two opposing forces—good and evil, God and Satan, Heaven and Hell. The myth of the Fall of Satan from God is interpreted in an entirely different way by Lawrence in some of his last poems.

In Lawrence's view, Satan did not fall from God because he became so proud and lofty that he wanted to challenge God as his equal. Rather, it was because God was getting too high and mighty, making it essential for some balancing of his power and life to take place. Satan separated from God in order to make more room for human beings to feel free from the fear of God. Thus they could enjoy the lovely things of nature during their earthly journey without the overwhelming pressure of patriarchal perfection always bearing down on them. Here is the poem, "When Satan Fell" which contains a deeper wisdom than the original biblical myth.

> *When Satan fell, he only fell*
> *because the Lord Almighty rose a bit too high,*
> *a bit beyond himself.*
>
> *So Satan only fell to keep a balance.*
> *"Are you so lofty, O my God?*
> *Are you so pure and lofty, up aloft?*
> *Then I will fall, and plant the paths to hell*
> *with vines and poppies and fig trees*
> *so that lost souls may eat grapes*
> *and the moist fig*
> *and put scarlet buds in their hair on the way to hell,*
> *on the way to dark perdition."*

And heaven and hell are the scales of the balance of life

> *which swing against each other.*

So for Lawrence, evil is not a metaphysical reality or cosmic force seeking to destroy the work of God in the life of man. It is rather a quality of human life, something we ourselves create as a result of decisions we make about the way we live our lives and choose our values. Of course, we are heavily, almost overwhelmingly, influenced in our choices by the world around us. What our society admires and values is what we strive for whether it is truly worthwhile or not, and in that, we fall into evil.

According to Lawrence the world's values can be best symbolized and imaged by the wheel. The mechanical revolving of our lives around the hub of the human ego is the very wheel which is the image of evil. Making the conscious self the very center of life and seeking to avoid all the experiences which might take us out of ourselves, shake us up, get us out of our comfort zone of self-satisfied circular existence - this is the essence of evil.

And the locus of this evil is the human soul and its will, turning round and round itself like a wheel round its hub. In a poem entitled "What Then Is Evil?" this is made painfully clear:

> Oh, in the world of the flesh of man
> iron gives the deadly wound
> and the wheel starts the principle of evil.
>
> Oh, in the world of things
> the wheel is the first principle of evil.
>
> But in the world of the soul of man
> there, and there alone lies the pivot of pure evil
> only in the soul of man, when it pivots upon the ego.
>
> When the mind of man makes a wheel which turns on the
>   hub of the ego
> and the will, the living dynamo, gives the motion and the
> speed
> and the wheel of the conscious self spins on in absolution,
> absolute
> absolute, absolved from the sun and the earth and the moon,
> absolute consciousness, absolved from strife and kisses
> absolute self-awareness, absolved from the meddling of
> creation
> absolute freedom, absolved from the great necessities of being

then we see evil, pure evil
and we see it only in man
and in his machines.

In other words, pure evil lies in our efforts to transcend our humanity, run from our vulnerability, reduce our exposure to life, and use our knowledge, skill, and invented machines as protective devices rather than as means of deepening, broadening, and intensifying our contact with the pulsing, challenging, and yes, painful, life all around us.

So, we go around in a wheel-like circle of self-concern, self-involvement, and self-aggrandizement. We separate ourselves from nature (the sun, the earth, the moon); we separate ourselves from human relationships (strife and kisses); we try to avoid the meddling of creation and the necessities of being, and rise above them all in a kind of whirling grandiosity. Is it any wonder that Lawrence chose the wheel as his image of pure evil?

Well, what is the opposite of this wheel-like way of existence? If we go beyond it, won't we be bucking the tide of reality? Isn't it true, for example that everything goes around in a circle? Look at the solar system, the revolving of the earth around the sun, the orbits of the heavenly bodies? Don't the very movements of the universe resemble a wheeling circular motion?

Lawrence stays a step ahead of this kind of justification of circular evil. He claims that the universe is not static and circular, but moving constantly ahead, going somewhere all the time, onwards into un-traveled space. He spells this out for us in "The Wandering Cosmos":

Oh, do not tell me the heavens as well are a wheel.
For every revolution of the earth around the sun
is a footstep onwards, onwards, we know not whither
and we do not care,

but a step onwards in untravelled space,
for the earth, like the sun, is a wanderer.

Their going round each time is a step
onwards, we know not whither,
but onwards, onwards, for the heavens are wandering
the moon and the earth, the sun, Saturn and Betelgeuse,
     Vega and Sirius and Altair,
they wander their strange and different ways in heaven
past Venus and Uranus and the signs.

For life is a wandering, we know not whither, but going.

Only the wheel goes round, but it never wanders.
     It stays on its hub.

If Lawrence had known about the red-shift discovery in astronomy which shows that all the galaxies are moving away from each other at inconceivable rates of speed, it certainly would have confirmed him in his conviction that the cosmos is indeed *wandering*. And if he had known about some of the modern scientific philosopher's descriptions of the universe as *a creative advance into novelty,* he would have sung for joy.

Of course, all these images are metaphorical - the wheel and the wanderer - and the metaphors are speaking Lawrence's truth and experience about human life. He had seen far too many of his contemporaries caught up in the wheels of the industrial revolution and, worse yet, the wheels of World War I. The mechanization of human existence was to him the most devilish movement of history. He spent his life seeking to counter-balance the dangers of this de-humanizing trend.

His novels and poems were all singing forth a different melody, proclaiming a different message, namely that the inwardness of human life must at all costs be preserved. Its imaginations, feelings, impulses, intuitions, and passions must be affirmed and celebrated in a thousand ways, over and over. In literature, in poetry, in art, and through every pliable medium, human life must be honored and revered. For just as the human soul is the source of evil; it is also the fountain of goodness, truth, and beauty.

Recovery from evil must begin in the human being's commitment to depart from the endless repetition of ego-centered behavior. We must surrender our efforts at making ourselves invulnerable to the changes and chances of life.

Then, we must together create islands of vibrant, adventurous, creative life, nurture them and guard them from the intrusions of the mechanistic, wheel-driven world. Lawrence lays down the gauntlet of challenge for us in his short poem "Departure."

> *Now some men must get up and depart*
> *from evil, or all is lost.*
>
> *...*
>
> *Evil is upon us and has got hold of us.*
> *Men must depart from it, or all is lost.*
> *We must make an isle impregnable*
> *against evil.*

Maybe this challenge of Lawrence's falls a little short of being truly helpful. But it is a start, the sound of a trumpet, and that is the encouragement we desperately need.

Facing Into Death

Self Pity

I never saw a wild thing
sorry for itself.
A small bird will drop frozen dead from a bough
without ever having felt sorry for itself.

So Let Me Live

So let me live that I may die
eagerly passing over from the entanglement of life
to the adventure of death, in eagerness
turning to death as I turn to beauty,
to the breath, that is, of new beauty unfolding in death.

Gladness Of Death

Oh death
about you I know nothing, nothing—
about the afterwards
as a matter of fact, we know nothing.

Yet oh death, oh death
also I know so much about you,
the knowledge is within me, without being a matter of fact.

And so I know
after the painful, painful experience of dying
there comes an after gladness, a strange joy
in a great adventure
oh the great adventure of death, where Thomas Cook cannot
          guide us.
...
Men prevent one another from being men
but in the great spaces of death
the winds of the afterwards kiss us into the blossom of manhood.

In Trouble And Shame

   I look at the swaling sunset
   And wish I could go also
Through the red doors beyond the black-purple bar.

   I wish that I could go
Through the red doors where I could put off
   My shame like shoes in the porch,
   My pain like garments,

And leave my flesh discarded lying
Like luggage of some departed traveler
Gone one knows not whither.

Then I would turn round,
And seeing my cast-off body lying like lumber,
I would laugh with joy.

Grudge Of The Old

The old ones want to be young, and they aren't young,
and it rankles, they ache when they see the young,
and they can't help wanting to spite it on them venomously.

The old ones say to themselves: We are not going to be old,
we are not going to make way, we are not going to die,
we are going to stay on and on and on and on and on
and make the young look after us
till they are old.

Shadows

...
And if, in the changing phases of man's life
I fall in sickness and misery
my wrists seem broken and my heart seems dead
and strength is gone, and my life
is only the leavings of a life:

*and still, among it all, snatches of lovely oblivion, and snatches of
      renewal
odd, wintry flowers upon the withered stem, yet new, strange
      flowers
such as my life has not brought forth before, new blossoms of me—*

*then I must know that still
I am in the hands of the unknown God,
he is breaking me down to his own oblivion
to send me forth on a new morning, a new man.*

Phoenix

*Are you willing to be sponged out, erased, cancelled,
made nothing?
Are you willing to be made nothing?
dipped into oblivion?*

If not, you will never really change.

*The phoenix renews her youth
only when she is burnt, burnt alive, burnt down
to hot and flocculent ash.
Then the small stirring of a new small bub in the nest
with strands of down like floating ash
shows that she is renewing her youth like the eagle,
immortal bird.*

How each human being deals with the inescapable event of death
reveals more about his/her character than any other one thing.
Death is at once an unfathomable mystery and a blatant fact.

Facing it consciously is a hallmark of our humanity. In a short poem entitled "Self-Pity," Lawrence writes:

I never saw a wild thing
sorry for itself.
A small bird will drop frozen dead from a bough
without ever having felt sorry for itself.

Wild things are not cursed with the gift of consciousness, so they never enter the realm of anxiety about mortality which humans have to live in. Men and women, being blessed with consciousness, bear a burden unique to their species, namely, the awareness that one day they will cease to be and will forever disappear from the face of the earth.

D.H. Lawrence had to face this fact earlier in life than most. He contracted what proved to be tuberculosis at around thirty-five years of age and the disease slowly took his life over the next ten years. His first response to this discovery was denial. He refused to believe his respiratory distress was anything more than bronchitis. "I've had bronchitis since I was a child, it's nothing new," was his typical reaction.

This denial scheme also kept him from getting help from sources of professional medicine. He chose to believe that all he needed was to get into a better environment for breathing. So he moved often, not just from wanderlust, but also for a supposed advantage for his bronchitis. His love for the little town of Taos in the high desert country of New Mexico, with its low humidity and bright sunshine, was in part due to its positive effect on his health.

Ultimately, he had to face into death. Much of his poetry was written during the last eighteen months of his life as he convalesced in one of his other favorite places, the mountains of northern Italy. Some of these poems contain remarkable visions and affirmations about the final stage of the human journey. These poems fall within a spectrum from hope to despair.

For example, an expression of hope comes forth in "So Let Me Live."

> *So let me live that I may die*
> *eagerly passing over from the entanglement of life*
> *to the adventure of death, in eagerness*
> *turning to death as I turn to beauty*
> *to the breath, that is, of new beauty unfolding in death.*

One poem is even titled "Gladness Of Death." It at first contains a confession of ignorance about the last mystery, but then moves into a pose of supposed intuitive knowledge, ending in the affirmation that death brings human life to its full fruition:

> *Oh death*
> *about you I know nothing, nothing—*
> *about the afterwards*
> *as a matter of fact, we know nothing.*
> *Yet oh death, oh death*
> *also I know so much about you,*
> *the knowledge is within me, without being a matter of fact.*
>
> *And so I know*
> *after the painful, painful experience of dying*
> *there comes an after gladness, a strange joy*
> *in a great adventure*
> *oh the great adventure of death,*
> > *where Thomas Cook cannot guide us.*

From this clever mention of Thomas Cook, the famous travel writer in Great Britain, the poem rambles on to a final verse affirming the faith that after death we begin to be free of hindrances and to become our great, true selves.

> *Men prevent one another from being men*

but in the great spaces of death
the winds of the afterwards kiss us into the blossom of manhood.

These poems come from Lawrence's later days and represent some of his more careful reflection. However, his very first poem about death was written in his early twenties. His mother had died recently and this had thrown him into a deep, even suicidal depression. His attachment to his mother had all the marks of a classic oedipal relationship and though her death was to free him up for greater maturity, its first effect was to devastate him emotionally and physically. Some of his poems from this early time express his lonely yearning to join his mother in death.

As he gazed one evening at the sunset and watched it sinking slowly into the banks of red and purple clouds lying on the western horizon, it stirred in him the desire to enter the eternal world through the beckoning colors of the sunset. So, the poem "In Trouble And Shame" expresses both his desire and joy at the possibility of following his mother home.

I look at the swaling sunset
And wish I could go also
Through the red doors beyond the black-purple bar.

I wish that I could go
Through the red doors where I could put off
My shame like shoes in the porch,
My pain like garments,
And leave my flesh discarded lying
Like luggage of some departed traveler
Gone one knows not whither.

Then I would turn round,
And seeing my cast-off body lying like lumber,
I would laugh with joy.

This is a poetic affirmation of the survival of the human consciousness after death. In his later poems about death, his certainty about this matter gets qualified and the destiny of the human being is less clearly stated. His church upbringing, insisted on by his mother, shaped his thoughts much more definitely during his teens and twenties. Later on he rejected much of his Christian teaching and this made his image of death less triumphant and more nebulous.

So, what were his more mature convictions about man's final journey? For one thing, he believed there must be a careful and thorough preparation for the eventuality of death. The primary goal in this preparation was the overcoming of ego-centeredness. He makes a list of the defects he believes disqualifies one for the mysterious final journey: "the stiff-necked people, and the self-willed people, and self-important ones, the self-righteous, self-absorbed, all of them who wind their energy round the idea of themselves." ("Vengeance Is Mine") These are the people, he believed, who cut themselves off from the source of life, the tree of life, and therefore are only good to be ground up as fertilizer or manure to help enrich the tree of life for the benefit of others.

Resistance to growing old is one clear-cut expression of this ego-centric self-assertion. In his poem, "The Grudge Of The Old," he puts it so:

The old ones want to be young, and they aren't young,
and it rankles, they ache when they see the young,
and they can't help wanting to spite it on them
venomously.

The old ones say to themselves: We are not going to be old,
we are not going to make way, we are not going to die,
we are going to stay on and on and on and on and on
and make the young look after us
till they are old.

The other major part of preparation for death is to keep a growing edge, constantly renewing one's life, continuing to let life come to flower and fruition well into one's waning years. Even when good health is gone, one can trust that the divine creativity can still produce new beauty and grace. Lawrence's trust in this divine reality kept him growing and creating right up to the closing day of his life. The shadows of death are closing around him but he believed he was still in the hands of God. Here is a passage from his poem entitled "Shadows" which gives beautiful expression to his faith.

> *And if, in the changing phases of man's life*
> *I fall in sickness and misery*
> *my wrists seem broken and my heart seems dead*
> *and strength is gone, and my life*
> *is only the leavings of a life:*
>
> *and still, among it all, snatches of lovely oblivion, and*
> *snatches of renewal,*
> *odd, wintry flowers upon the withered stem, yet new, strange*
> *flowers*
> *such as my life has not brought forth before, new blossoms of*
> *me—*
>
> *then I must know that still*
> *I am in the hands [of] the unknown God,*
> *he is breaking me down to his own oblivion*
> *to send me forth on a new morning, a new man.*

The secret of this continuing re-creation is surrender of the ego's selfish grip on life. The willingness to let go and allow the journey to come to an end is what opens the way to the future of God's remaking of the dying person. One of Lawrence's final poems was called "Phoenix," recalling the legendary bird which immolates itself in order to be reborn a new and more beautiful creature. Here is how the final challenge is expressed.

Are you willing to be sponged out, erased, cancelled,
made nothing?
Are you willing to be made nothing?
dipped into oblivion?

If not, you will never really change.

The phoenix renews her youth
only when she is burnt, burnt alive, burnt down
to hot and flocculent ash.
Then the small stirring of a new small bub in the nest
with strands of down like floating ash
shows that she is renewing her youth like the eagle,
immortal bird.

The last lines of "Phoenix" express the hope of resurrection and the renewal of life in the midst of death. Lawrence's faith circled around this possibility of resurrection.. He was not so certain of the reality of a resurrection after death, but was deeply committed to the resurrection of the body during life.

One of his major criticisms of Christianity was its failure to make the image of the resurrection the dominant theme of its life and teaching and ritual. It was a mistake, he believed, to put so much emphasis on the Nativity with its images of the mother and the child. He was especially critical of the Roman Catholic doctrine of the sanctity of the Mother and the magical nature of the Child. He was convinced that the prominence of this image kept human beings thinking of themselves as children, dependent and adoring but essentially helpless in attempts to achieve real maturity of life and vitality.

At the same time he objected also to the image of Christ Crucified, the dramatic picture of the suffering savior of the world. This image, too, kept human beings in a dependent state, having to cling to the beneficence of a dying other as their only source of hope and life. While this image enabled people to transcend the Mother-image, it nonetheless fell short of the fullness of the truth about redemption.

It is only when the Resurrection is made the key and fundamental truth of religion that human beings receive the help they most need. In the story of the Risen Lord human beings are brought to the understanding that both the meaning of life and the conquest of death are grounded in the resurrection of the flesh.

It is while we are still in the flesh that our salvation must be made real. The resurrection of the flesh is the coming alive of the human being with creative vitality in the here and now. It is being flooded with energy from the other world, the "fourth dimension" as Lawrence sometimes put it that truly delivers one from deadness and death.

It was Lawrence's plea that humanity be open to the Risen Lord energy and thus experience their own resurrection of the flesh. Only in this way will human beings possess sufficient vitality to make a difference in this life or come to feel the hope of re-emergence in the next.

D.H. Lawrence was a great example of a human being facing into death in a highly conscious way. He accepted his own death as a growing part of his life and used himself up in the creative expression of his god-given gifts. He died in early March of 1930, in the presence of his wife, Frieda, and some close friends. He passed quietly and in peace, having left so much of himself behind that generations to come could feed upon his writings and poems, and thus make their own life journeys deeper and richer and their own facing of the final reality less lonely.

Appendix A

D(avid) H(erbert) Lawrence (1885-1930)

Petri Liukkonen

English novelist, story writer, critic, poet and painter, one of the greatest figures in 20th-century English literature, Lawrence saw sex and intuition as a key to undistorted perception of reality and a way to respond to the inhumanity of the industrial culture. From Lawrence's doctrines of sexual freedom arose obscenity trials, which had a deep effect on the relationship between literature and society. In 1912 he wrote: "What the blood feels, and believes, and says, is always true." Lawrence's life after World War I was marked with continuous and restless wandering.

> "The novel is the book of life. In this sense, the Bible is a great confused novel. You may say, it is about God. But it is really about man alive. Adam, Eve, Sarai, Abraham, Isaac, Jacob, Samuel, David, Bath-sheba, Ruth, Esther, Solomon, Job, Isaiah, Jesus, mark, Judas, Paul, Peter: what is it but man alive, from start to finish? Man alive, not mere bits. Even the Lord is another man alive, in a burning bush, throwing the tablets of stone at Moses's head." (from 'Why the Novel Matters' in *D.H. Lawrence: Selected Criticism*, 1956)

David Herbert Lawrence was born in Eastwood, Nottinghamshire, in central England. He was the fourth child of a struggling coal miner who was a heavy drinker. His mother was a former schoolteacher, greatly superior in education to her husband. Lawrence's childhood was dominated by poverty and friction between his parents. In a letter from 1910 to the poet Rachel Annand Taylor he later wrote: "Their marriage life has been one carnal, bloody fight. I was born hating my father: as early as ever I can remember, I shivered with horror when he touched me. He was very bad before I was born." Encouraged by his mother, with whom he had a deep emotional bond and who figures as Mrs. Morel in his first masterpiece, Lawrence became interested in arts. He was educated at Nottingham High School, to which he had won a scholarship. He worked as a clerk in a surgical appliance factory and then four years as a pupil-teacher. After studies at Nottingham University, Lawrence received his teaching certificate at 22 and briefly pursued a teaching career at Davidson Road School in Croydon in South London (1908-1911). Lawrence's mother died in 1910—he helped her die by giving her an overdose of sleeping medicine. This scene was re-created in his novel *Sons and Lovers*.

In 1909 a number of Lawrence's poems were submitted by Jessie Chambers, his childhood sweetheart, to Ford Madox Ford, who published them in *English Review*. The appearance of his first novel, *The White Peacock*, launched Lawrence as a writer at the age of 25. In 1912 he met Frieda von Richthofen, the professor Ernest Weekly's wife and fell in love with her. Frieda left her husband and three children, and they eloped to Bavaria and then continued to Austria, Germany and Italy. In 1913 Lawrence's novel *Sons and Lovers* appeared, which was based on his childhood and contains a portrayal of Jessie Chambers, the Miriam in the novel and called 'Muriel' in early stories. When the book was rejected by Heinemann, Lawrence wrote to his friend: "Curse the blasted, jelly-boned swines, the slimy, the belly-wriggling invertebrates, the miserable sodding rutters, the flaming sods, the sniveling, dribbling, dithering, palsied, pulse-less lot that make up England today."

In 1914 Lawrence married Frieda von Richthofen, and traveled with her in several countries in the final two decades of his life. Lawrence's fourth novel, *The Rainbow* (1915), was about two sisters growing up in the north of England. The character of Ursula Brangwen was partly based on Lawrence's teacher associate in Nottingham, Louie Burrows. She was Lawrence's first love. The novel was banned for its alleged obscenity—it used swear words and talked openly about sex. Lawrence's frankness in describing sexual relations between men and women upset a great many people and over 1,000 copies of the novel were burned by the examining magistrate's order. The banning created further difficulties for him in getting anything published. Also his paintings were confiscated from an art gallery. John Middleton Mutty and Catherine Mansfield offered Lawrence their various 'little magazines' for his texts. An important patron was Lady Ottoline Morrell, wife of a Liberal Member of Parliament. Through her, Lawrence formed relationships with several cultural figures, among them Aldous Huxley, E.M. Forster, and Bertrand Russell, with whom he was later to quarrel bitterly.

During the First World War Lawrence and his wife were unable to obtain passports and were target of constant harassment from the authorities. Frieda, a cousin of the legendary "Red Baron" von Richthofen, was viewed with great suspicion. They were accused of spying for the Germans and officially expelled from Cornwall in 1917. The Lawrences were not permitted to emigrate until 1919, when their years of wandering began.

Lawrence started to write *The Lost Girl* (1920) in Italy. He had settled with Frieda in Gargano. In those days they were so poor that they could not afford even a newspaper. The novel dealt with one of Lawrence's favorite subjects—a girl marries a man of a much lower social status, against the advice of friends, and finds compensation in his superior warmth and understanding. "But it needs a certain natural gift to become a loose woman or a prostitute. If you haven't got the qualities which attract loose men, what are you to do?

Supposing it isn't in your nature to attract loose and promiscuous men! Why, then you can't be a prostitute, if you try your head off: nor even a loose woman. Since *willing* won't do it. It requires a second party to come to an agreement." (from *The Lost Girl*, 1920) Lawrence dropped the novel for some years and rewrote the story in an old Sicilian farm-house near Taormina in 1920.

In the 1920s Aldous Huxley traveled with Lawrence in Italy and France. Between 1922 and 1926 he and Frieda left Italy to live intermittently in Ceylon, Australia, New Mexico, and Mexico. These years provided settings for several of Lawrence's novels and stories. In 1924 the New York socialite Mabel Dodge Luhan gave to Lawrence and Frieda the Kiowa Ranch in Taos, receiving in return the original manuscript of *Sons and Lovers*. In an essay called 'New Mexico' (1928) Lawrence wrote that "New Mexico was the greatest experience from the outside world that I have ever had." He felt that it liberated him from the present era of civilization—"a new part of the soul woke up suddenly, and the old world gave way to a new." After severe illness in Mexico, it was discovered that he was suffering from life-threatening tuberculosis. From 1925 the Lawrences confined their travels to Europe.

Lawrence's best known work is *Lady Chatterley's Lover*, first published privately in Florence in 1928. It tells of the love affair between a wealthy, married woman, Constance Chatterley, and a man who works on her husband's estate. A war wound has left her husband, Sir Clifford, a mine owner in Derbyshire, impotent and paralyzed. Constance has a brief affair with a young playwright and then enters into a passionate relationship with Sir Clifford's gamekeeper, Oliver Melloers. Connie becomes pregnant. Sir Clifford refuses to give a divorce and the lovers wait for better time when they could be united. "Necessary, forever necessary, to burn out false shames and smelt the heaviest ore of the body into purity." —One of the models for the cuckolder-gamekeeper was Angelino Ravagli, who received half the Lawrence estate after Frieda's death.

Lady Chatterley's Lover was banned for a time in both the UK and the US as pornographic. In the UK it was published in unexpurgated form in 1960 after an obscenity trial, where defense witnesses included E.M. Forster, Helen Gardner, and Richard Hoggart. Lawrence's other novels from the 1920s include *Women in Love* (1920), a sequel to *Rainbow*. The characters are probably partially based on Lawrence and his wife, and John Middleton Murray and his wife Katherine Mansfield. The friends shared a house in England in 1914-15. Lawrence used the English composer and songwriter Philip Heseltine as the basis for Julius Halliday, who never forgave it. When a manuscript of philosophical essays by Lawrence fell into Heseltine's hands—no other copies of the text existed—he used it as toilet tissue. According to an anecdote, Lawrence never trusted the opinions of Murray and when Murray told that he believed that there was no God, Lawrence replied, "Now I know there is."

Lawrence argued that instincts and intuitions are more important than the reason. "Instinct makes me run from little over-earnest ladies; instinct makes me sniff the lime blossom and reach for the darkest cherry. But it is intuition which makes me feel the uncanny glassiness of the lake this afternoon, the sulkiness of the mountains, the vividness of near green in thunder-sun, the young man in bright blue trousers lightly tossing the grass from the scythe, the elderly man in a boater stiffly shoving his scythe strokes, both of them sweating in the silence of the intense light." (from 'Insouciance', 1928) Lawrence's belief in the importance of instincts reflected the thought of Friedrich Nietzsche, whom Lawrence had read already in the 1910s. *Aaron's Road* (1922) shows directly the influence of Nietzsche, and in *Kangaroo* (1923) Lawrence expressed his own idea of a 'superman'. *The Plumed Serpent* (1926) was a vivid evocation of Mexico and its ancient Aztec religion. *The Man Who*

Died (1929), first published under the title *The Escaped Cock*, was a bold version of the story of Christ's resurrection. Instead of having Christ go to heaven, Lawrence has him mate with the priestess of Isis. Lawrence's non-fiction works include *Movements in European History* (1921), *Psychoanalysis and the Unconcious* (1922), *Studies in Classic American Literature* (1923) and *Apocalypse and the Writings on Revelation* (1931).

D.H. Lawrence died in Vence, France on March 2, 1930. Frieda (d. 1956) moved to the Kiowa Ranch and built a small memorial chapel to Lawrence; his ashes lie there. In 1950 she married Angelino Ravagli, a former Italian infantry officer, with whom she had started an affair in 1925. Jake Zeitlin, a Los Angeles bookseller, who first took care of Lawrence's literary estate, summarized his feeling when he first saw the author's manuscripts: "That night when I first opened the trunk containing the manuscripts of Lawrence and as I looked through them, watched unfold the immense pattern of his vision and the tremendous product of his energy, there stirred in me an emotion similar to that I felt when first viewing the heavens with a telescope."

Lawrence also gained posthumous renown for his expressionistic paintings completed in the 1920s.

Appendix B

Partial Bibliography of D.H. Lawrence's Works

The following bibliography contains only the novels, volumes of poetry and selected non-fiction of D.H. Lawrence. It does not include short stories, letters, and other critical writings.

Publication Date	Title
1911	*The White Peacock*
1912	*The Trespasser*
1913	*Sons and Lovers*
	Love Poems and Others
1915	*The Rainbow*
1916	*Amores*
1917	*Look! We Have Come Through!*
1918	*New Poems*
1919	*Bay: A Book of Poems*
1920	*The Lost Girl*
	Women in Love
1921	*Tortoises*
	Movements in European History
	Psychoanalysis and the Unconscious
	Sea and Sardinia
1922	*Aaron's Rod*
	Fantasia of the Unconscious
1923	*Kangaroo*
	Birds, Beasts and Flowers
	Studies in Classic American Literature
1924	*The Boy in the Bush*
1926	*The Plumed Serpent*
1927	*Mornings in Mexico*
1928	*Lady Chatterley's Lover*
	The Collected Poems of D. H. Lawrence

1929   *The Escaped Cock (aka The Man Who Died)*
Pansies
The Paintings of D. H. Lawrence

1930   *The Virgin and the Gypsy*
Nettles

1931   *Apocalypse and the Writings on Revelation*

1932   *Last Poems*

1936   *Phoenix: the Posthumous Papers of D. H. Lawrence*

1940   *Fire and Other poems*

1964   *The Complete Poems of D. H. Lawrence*

About the Author

Don Jones, at 76, has had a long life of spiritual leadership including years serving as a pastor and preacher, helping youth and adults as executive director of non-profit organizations, teaching seminars in the field of Jungian psychology, and healing souls as a psychotherapist.

For the past fifteen years he has served as a Certified Leader of men's initiation weekends within The ManKind Project, an international organization whose mission is "to empower men to missions of service." He convened the first National Elder Council meeting of this men's order and completed a term as International Chairman of The ManKind Project.

He has written an earlier book of his own proverbs entitled *Wisdom For The Journey* and also published a yearly calendar of proverbs. These works are available for order on his website at http://www.twosnakespublishing.com.

He lives in Indianapolis, Indiana, with his wife Emily Hurst-Jones and two cats, Katie and Serena.

Printed in the United States
89930LV00003B/191/A